SEX WITHOUT MARRIAGE

SEX WITHOUT MARRIAGE

BONNIE GOLIGHTLY &
JONATHAN STARR

CUTTING EDGE

ISBN-13: 978-1-970848-17-5

Published by
Cutting Edge Books
PO Box 8212
Calabasas, CA 91372
www.cuttingedgebooks.com

FOREWORD

THE FIRST thing every tyro newspaperman learns is that each story has as its essentials a Who, What, When, Where and Why. These, the famous Five W's of newspaper reporting, can be applied to the story of sex; this book is such an application. Herein are the Who, What, When, Where and Why of Single Sex. There is no attempt within these Five W's to moralize; neither is there any attempt to temporize. The authors rather have stated the facts of sex life as they know them to be, garnished with their own opinions as they have developed them from their own considerable experience. A lot of people won't like this book. These are the people who don't like Life, as it exists in reality, either.

This book wasn't written for them. It was written for you.

——The Authors

PART ONE

CHAPTER ONE

WHAT IT'S ALL ABOUT

THE SEX life of the sophisticated and single American male may, in a number of ways, be likened to the Fourth of July. Both, for example, are continuing indications of independence; idylically, each will be safe and sane, if somewhat explosive; both occasions, of course, offer the single man an excuse to bang the drums and toot the horns—an emotional opening of the safety valve. However, there is also this essential difference to be noted: Independence Day comes but once a year. It is devoutly to be wished that the single man will taste of the nectar that is woman more than once a year.

Perhaps this is, after all, an essay toward that exact end. A kind of, what-to, when-to and with-who-to that will increase the success ratio of your boudoir forays, that will increase the frequency, as they say, of your "times at bat."

Sex. Over the centuries billions of words have been lavished on the subject. Artists and writers have been inspired by it. Empires have risen and fallen because of it. Thrones have been surrendered, lives have been enriched by it. Curses have been heaped upon it.

People like it.

Dr. Kinsey and other notable researchers have underscored this basic fact of life among the American males and females. They like sex. They enjoy sex. They partake of sex. Nothing that will be said or could be said on these pages will alter that fact. To attempt here a message of morality therefore is more than merely beyond the scope or intent of the author; it would be presumption. Indeed, sanctimony.

Instead, viewing the American single male with dispassionate objectivity, the author seeks to hack away at the tangled undergrowth of rose-colored hypocrisy that chokes so many roads to truth, smoothing thereby the path the single man already has elected to follow.

Why is this task even necessary? So who needs it?

You do, as I once did, and still do once in a while to remind myself of who I am, who they are, and what should be done about it. And it's all because in our society more time is spent contemplating sex, talking sex, reading sex and reaming sex than doing it. Part of this is due the peculiar American tradition of placing the American female on a pedestal. I have news for you. She doesn't like it up there. She was put there by men who never knew her, and she's just waiting for the man to come along who can bring her back down to earth where she belongs.

You are that man. It's up to you to help her. Theories can be beautiful, but they're even more beautiful executed with intelligence and vigor. This, then, is an attempt to apply that good old Yankee know-how to one of the most fascinating areas of daily living.

Statistics prove that many of our young men are unfit physically for military service, being flabby of both mind and body. Too often one hears from women that:

"Men are weak."

"There are few men and many boys."

"A woman must take charge since the man won't."

All these complaints seem to have a sound basis. Men appear to have abdicated their traditional masculine role. Too often they have become second rate lovers, able to set a woman up for the knockout punch but unable to deliver it. The result is unsatisfying evenings and long and lonely nights. A deplorable situation. Something must be done.

"Le plaisir de l'amour est d'aimer," said La Rochefoucauld, with all the typical disarming frankness of the French. "The pleasure of love is in the loving."

Who can deny it? It's all very well to talk about playing the game for the game's sake, but I put that down as a rationale for losers. Winners play to win!

The choice then is simple, to win or to lose. And since the race is run against yourself you have it in you to be either. You say you want to be a winner? Very well. Then it is necessary to bring your considerable intelligence to bear on the subject. Accept the reality of it. Here we have a fundamental desire, nay, a need, of all people, a physical and emotional craving which has been roped and hogtied with cerebral maunderings until few of us know what it's all about. Women frequently don intellectual chastity belts for which you must find the key.

Understand what it's all about. Which of us has not been distressed, after cocktails at Four Seasons, dinner at Pablo's, the theatre and then a brandy at the Harwyn, to discover that he and his companion do not speak the same language? That they are playing different games, or, worse yet, the same game but with different rules? It ruins what began as a hell of an evening.

Let's put things right. Single sex is a fact of life. Women accept it as such. They may fight it, obstruct it, delay it, ignore it, refuse it and confuse it, but they never deny it. Men, however, often act in a fashion quite unfathomable. They perform socially as if the urging of their libidos was a siren call to disaster. Men have been known to actually deny an interest in the subject! Yes, it's true. Believe it. Such guilt, on both an individual and collective basis, is appalling. For a man to place himself in such an odious position, to come hatin-hand, denying his very nature, is enough to repel any ripe and lusty female. It is no wonder that young women often prefer older men who suavely go about their business.

I grant that given the time you may learn all the information packed into the following pages for yourself. It is my earnest hope, however, to speed up the process for you, to ease the pain of repeated falls from social grace. Don't talk about it, do it.

To deal with contemporary females one must act from a position of strength. Strength comes from knowledge. Knowledge breeds success. Success begets confidence which in turn begets more success. In these pages I shall attempt to impart to you knowledge gained from both personal experience as well as academic research. Study this information, absorb it as a sponge does water, make it a part of yourself. You must learn to act right, think right, trusting your instincts, which will be sharpened with practice and achievement. Remember, you are truly a unique creation, as each of us is, and so your own personality, your own strong points must color everything you do and say. Learn to like yourself. It may be hard at first, since you know yourself better than anyone else, but try. If you like you, someone else may get the idea. Believe me, it helps. And so to the business at hand …

The name of the game is lechery.

Many people shudder at the word. Don't. There is no need. It is an honest word, long in use. It's traditions are well established, reaching back into the dawn of pre-history when the more carnal cavemen lured hirsute beauties into their lairs. On what pretext? To see their wall drawings, of course.

The Ancient Greek was a lot smoother. An idealist and true sophisticate, he was warrior and athlete, artist and philosopher, political theorist and lover. He lived life fully, enjoying every facet of it, for despite his sophistication his everyday behavior and ideals were based on simple and sensual Hedonism. The whole of Greek life was in praise of pleasure, of life *in general,* of sensual pursuits. The poet Simonides said, "Would the life of mortals be delightful without sensual happiness?" Thus the desire of male for female rather than being frowned upon was indulged approvingly for what it was, a healthy manifestation of man's lust for life. The Greeks excluded sex from no portion of their existence, not even their religious rites. Their orgiastic practices were controlled, soundly motivated excursions during which they paid their respects to the gods.

As in all things, the Romans sought to emulate the Greeks. But, as in the arts, they were only copyists, able to produce nothing new.

Warriors have remained in the public eye long beyond their own lifetimes. Such as Caesar, Hannibal, Napoleon, Richard the Lion Hearted, and the rest, all cut colorful figures. But there are lovers, both fictional and factual, who are equally long-lived: Don Juan, Lothario, Casanova, Romeo, Paris, to mention a few. Nor are the great romancers confined to antiquity. John Garfield was in the company of a lady when the end came. What better way to go? And Errol Flynn expired a contented, though undoubtedly weary, fellow. Surely the mention of such illustrious names will evoke a sigh of regret over what is over and done with in many a boudoir across the land. Can any full-blooded male aspire to less?

To a large degree, a man's success with women may be measured accurately by his ambition. The greater the latter the greater the former. The one who seeks to exceed his grasp may very well tumble onto his face, but he may also get what he wants. Not to try is to insure failure. Such cowardice on the field of combat is intolerable. It must be eradicated.

You will hear it said often that the battle of the sexes is a myth. That men and women are essentially compatible, and so they are. However, superficially they fight like alley cats, each striving to attain a position of superiority. One of the major social problems in our society is the competitive aspect of women, and man's frequent surrender to it.

This has come into being by means of a subtle psychological transfer of responsibilities and dependencies. The struggle of women to gain the vote snowballed into a general power play which brought them more and more into what had heretofore been a man's world. More and more women took over jobs that men had handled, and in some cases were better suited to the work. In the past women remained at home while men roamed the jungle in search of meat, or a pay envelope. Now there are few women unequipped to provide for themselves economically. Thus has man's position been undercut, and he has in few ways seen fit to compensate. Women have become his equal and they often find it difficult, if not downright impossible, to submit, no matter how much they would like to. Aware of this desperate state of affairs, the competent lecher will adapt himself accordingly. Later chapters will discuss the approach to and conquest of The Predator, among other types of seemingly self-sufficient females.

It is worth noting that the native lecher functions under a depressing handicap, which doesn't affect his European brother. He springs out of a long and honorable tradition which serves as an excellent perspective for his activities. This frame of reference provides sustenance and moral strength. Not so the American gallant. What Yankee doodler can shake off that rigid Puritanical history of ours with its threats of damnation and witch hunting and invocations of hellfire? Publicly, the land of the free ain't for the sexually brave; it brooks no deviation from the straight and narrow, though it tolerates, in fact, engenders, private falls from grace. The result, quite naturally, is a moral ambivalence that confuses the young, undermines the purposeful, destroys the resolute. The result—a strikeout! To the would-be successful lecher, these words of advice: accentuate the positive, eliminate the negative, latch on to the affirmative, don't mess with nothing in between.

Obviously some men require less sexual activity than others. This in no way lessens their need for a primer of beds and broads. To loosely paraphrase Marx (not Groucho or Harpo): From each according to his ability, to each according to his need.

Stay away from comparisons. Don't set yourself up at someone else's expense. To do so may reveal more of your own inadequacies than you intended. No yardsticks exist, except subjective ones, for plumbing the depths of another man's pleasure. It's not how much but how good.

A man may not desire feminine companionship frequently, but when he wants it he wants it. The trick is to be able to find it with a minimum of complication and a maximum of satisfaction. The question naturally arises where does one find women, and a following chapter deals with this situation, suggesting behavior patterns that fit individual environments. Since women may be encountered everywhere but in those few locations which are prohibited to them by decorum, if not tradition, it is necessary to list them by major categories, the most likely meeting places.

So is it with the women themselves. They abound in endless variety, a fact which makes it difficult for a man, like the proverbial kid in the candy factory, to make up his mind. To simplify matters, the author has segregated the American female into several dominating groups, groups established not arbitrarily but in terms of action and reaction, aiming directly at the desired result. These groupings are created with due consideration to differences of job classification, education, cultural interests, talents, hobbies, intelligence quotient, personality, beauty, physical dimensions and degree of promiscuity.

The key word for the seeker of single sex is attitude. Both his and his intended. It is vital, repeat *vital,* that one quickly recognize the category to which a target female belongs (which also means the category in which *she* thinks she belongs), and at the same time display an awareness of her individuality. All females give off signals. The perceptive male is able to tune in on them. To fail to read them loud and clear is to court utter disaster. An apt example comes to mind.

The flashing tail lights of the common firefly are part of a communication system. The female summons a passing male by signalling to him at the proper time interval, after he has dispatched his own blinking message. Possessing extra-large eyes (so as to see her signal better?), he zooms in to a smooth landing on the leaf beside her.

Now here is where attitude plays such an important role. Sometimes that flashing female invites a male who is not of her own kind. Her timing may have been off and she simply sent her signal on the wrong wave length, the frequency band of another species. She doesn't dig the panting male on her leaf, a fact which generally costs him his life. To her, a firefly who isn't a lover is merely a meal. Attitude, is everything.

In keeping with this, perhaps the biggest fundamental difference between the man who is highly successful with women and one who is not rests in their feelings toward women. The latter merely likes women, finding their company agreeable, any rewards one may bestow upon him he accepts with equanimity. Not so the former. He *loves* women. He *treasures* them. *Cherishes* them. Without their presence life would become intolerable, unthinkable. He finds real pleasure in girl-watching along Fifth Avenue; in the spring when the coats are discarded and all the evidence of femininity is once again on display, he comes alive. The sap of life boils over in him. He would rather dine with a woman than with a man, talk to one, walk with one, look at one. That fabled presence makes a movie play better, music sound richer, a painting more moving. They are the beginning and the end. All else is secondary.

He loves women.

One hears much of the fleshpots of Europe, of such lusty towns as Paris and Rome. The women there are different, you are told. Bigger, better, thinner, fatter, smaller, shorter, smarter, dumber, prettier, uglier, wiser, kinder. Don't you believe it. A girl is a girl is a girl. She may be striding along Madison Avenue in fashionable black, or flouncing flat-heeled across Main Street, Smalltown, U.S.A.; she may bounce along the Appian Way on a motor scooter, or just sit, or just walk, wherever you happen to spy her. It doesn't matter. She applies lip rouge one lip at a time. And 'No' is probably the first word she ever learned. It will be the last one she'll forget.

Unless you help her.

This then is an attempt to shorten and simplify the journey from desire to fulfillment. It won't help you when you get there. But then you must do something for yourself.

CHAPTER TWO

WHO THE GIRLS ARE ...

I N NEW YORK CITY unmarried women outnumber men on a three to two ratio. Like Hertz, this puts you in the driver's seat. The percentages may vary in different sections of the country, but not appreciably. In any case, there are certain specifics which work constantly to a man's advantage.

For example, the drive to get a man, to at least be going with someone, if not married, is a powerful force pushing almost every woman. She has been repeatedly hammered over the head since childhood with the need to win her own honest to goodness male and if she doesn't swing it, by gum, she can't amount to much. That's a pretty dirty trick to play on an unsuspecting girl, especially since we males know what small bargains most of us are. However, this is a show-them-no-mercy treatise. They have their troubles and we have ours.

The question, then, is how to recognize what particular neurosis a particular girl carries around with her, at the same time learning how to exploit it. In this day of packaged Freud, this is not difficult to accomplish. As a matter of fact, it is sometimes surprisingly simple. One need recognize certain significant indications. Before delving into the various feminine categories, I should like to treat briefly with the young woman in analysis or psychotherapy.

It is a reasonable assumption, reasonable enough to back with a small wager, that the next girl you meet at a cocktail party in New York or Chicago or any other metropolitan center will be in analysis. In fact, she'll probably tell you so. If you live in Faroutville, U.S.A., the odds are only a little longer. They actually may favor you. Since your townswoman may actually be in dire need of therapy and, not getting it, may find the word 'No' issues more slowly from her lips than it might.

Regardless, this girl, wherever you find her, is a creature unto herself. To begin with, she'll more than likely be a talker. She will gab on and on about herself and her problems. Tell her you're an advertising man and she will explain in a rational manner how advertising has corrupted the natural curve of her sex drive; mention that you sell shoes and be prepared for a monologue on her foot fetish. If you've got the strength and fortitude to wait the evening out this bit of disoriented fluff may invite you to share her bed, not out of passion but because it's such a friendly thing to do, like shaking hands or kissing goodnight. On the other hand, she may not.

Any female in any of the following groupings may be in analysis, in which case all bets are off, depending on the stage of the treatment. Remember, very often when a girl is under a doctor's care she will not make a move without his approval. This makes things a little tricky. Chances are that doctor is a man, so that in addition to not caring one whit about you (after all, she's his patient), he automatically knows every sneaky curve you're throwing the girl, every angle you're trying to exploit. And why not? He's probably tried them all himself.

Tread with caution then when the young lady puts you off with, "Phone me Thursday evening after eight." It simply means she's seeing her analyst between seven and eight, and believe me, that doctor is not on your side.

A case in point—a friend of mine, whom I shall call John, met Cynthia at a party. Soon afterwards she began recounting her adventures on the analyst's couch. John, a good listener, braced himself for the long haul. He took her to dinner at Michael's. With drinks the check was eighteen dollars. They decided to have a nightcap in the lounge of the Blue Angel. Then he hailed a cab and took her home. She lived in Queens. Three dollars and seventy-five cents worth of Queens, each way.

She said not tonight, John. Don't rush me, John. And because John is a good listener he listened and didn't act. She also told him to come around on Friday night when she was certain she'd be more receptive to him. John showed up at the appointed time to find her with her hair in curlers and cream on her face. Her doctor thought that casual sex at this time would prove self-defeating and she hoped John understood. John, being a good listener, understood. John rode back to Manhattan in a cab. Another three dollars and seventy-five cents. John is a jerk.

Don't you be.

THE OLDER WOMAN

In the lives of almost every man has come at least one Older Woman. She can prove to be something important, guiding and teaching you in a way that one of your contemporaries will never do. The coupling of a young man with a woman somewhat older is not generally a question of male conquest, no matter how desirable to one's ego this may seem. In fact, an Older Woman will usually decide when she wants a man, particularly one younger than herself. For invariably she will be wise enough to measure the situation accurately. She will not delude herself, as do her more callow sisters, that such a relationship can have lasting value.

With her more experienced and practical mind, she will be more inclined to accept life as it unfolds, taking what it has to offer and giving as she can. The young man who makes such a liaison is indeed fortunate. Convinced that he shares her bed because of his square jaw and powerful muscles, the average young man may fail to benefit from it, unless he can get his own ego out of the way. She will introduce him to the mysteries of love and love-making that come only with the years.

I met my Older Woman when I was in my early twenties. Looking back, I must wonder what she saw in me. Whatever it was, whatever need I was able to fill in her, I am grateful for it. She added a dimension to every facet of my life. She taught me that strength needn't be hardness, that only the strong can afford to be gentle; she forced me to look outside of myself, to involve myself in the life around me, to perceive more, to comprehend more, to feel more. She improved me for the women who came later. They never knew her but a part of me was always there when I visited them.

THE PREDATORS

Men are little more than *hors d'oeuvres* at a cocktail party for some women. They devour them and come back for more. Such man-eaters abound in the competitive social and business whirl in every metropolitan center. One can usually spot them from across the rim of a martini glass easily enough. Avoiding them is another story, and for good and sound reasons. They are generally fantastically attractive in every way.

By and large they are exceptionally good-looking, with well-turned figures. They dress tastefully and their makeup is never obtrusive. Most males are drawn to them like iron filings to a magnet. Having joined the group of similarly drawn young men-about-town surrounding such mantraps, one must fight to keep one's head above water. The scramble is on. The Predator does nothing to diminish the flow of blood. Rather she encouraged it by word and gesture until the wounded drift off bloody and bowed. She then takes the survivor in hand.

And very capable hands they are. They manipulate men as a puppeteer manipulates his dolls. You will be only too happy to wine and dine her in restaurants far beyond your income. You will pay scalper's prices for third row orchestra seats to hit musicals so she won't miss anything. You will lavish expensive gifts upon her because somehow it seems like the thing to do. You will lie curled up at her feet like a dog without spirit waiting for her to kick you. And she will.

Your lunch hours will be spent running her errands. Evenings you'll walk her dog while she dates someone else. When she goes on vacation you'll remain in the city on weekends in order to water her plants. And if she permits you the privilege of her body you'll pay for that too. For in a thousand small and demeaning ways she'll reduce you in stature until you've become a blurry, flabby figure of a man, the kind of man she cannot stomach, at which point she will unquetionably cast you out, informing you that she is now dating your best friend.

My advice is to keep your radar attuned for The Predator. She can do you no good. Initially, your ego may be somewhat inflated because of her attentions. You may be proud to take her to the theatre, or parties. It may please you when all heads turn as you enter a restaurant with her. But in the long run she will make less of you. She has turned off all feeling, buried all emotion, frozen all warmth. She will blame you for the weaknesses she aggravates, until, like that embittered firefly, she will devour you for not being the man she wants, the kind of man who could not possibly exist.

Firefly, fly.

THE QUICKIES

This grouping may by itself be broken down in a number of subdivisions. For simplicity's sake, I have arranged it under three headings. We begin with ...

The Virgin, whose presence in this grouping may startle you. How does it happen, you may well ask, does The Virgin find herself categorized with The Quickies? The answer, dear reader, is simple: it takes virtually no time at all to find out what she's all about. Or not about—to do.

Actually, The Virgin often saves one a considerable amount of time and effort on her own. She is given to volunteering broad hints about her own sleeping habits, which are often on her mind much more than the girl who is too busy bundling to reflect on it. Frequently The Virgin has the good taste to look, dress and act in accord with this do-nothing condition of hers. Some of them practically glow with Purity and Virtue. About these, few men need advice. Such females are generally colossal bores who repel men by the droves.

However, she has a sister-in-goodness who is a prime Time Waster. She is The Virgin who appears to ride the sexual bandwagon to social glory. She flirts outrageously. She talks sex incessantly. She makes lewd references to various parts of the body, anybody's body. She's a real 'Oh, You Kid, What You've Got In Store After The Party's Over' kind of girl. Forget it!

Sex is the carrot with which she leads innocent young males around. Why, she's so good that she even kisses with all the skill and passion of one who has actually been there. That should surprise no one, since she generally started playing this sneaky game quite early in life. The Time Waster will tell you with much sadness in her limpid eyes as her lips brush yours at her door, that she cannot invite you in because her roommate stays up late watching television (later the emasculating effects of That Diabolical Box will be explored in some detail). On the way home you'll choke back a sob, as you think of the girls in whose company you might have spent the evening. The entire evening.

These Professional Virgins are to be avoided. Learn to spot them quickly. One or two experiences with such insidious types will alert you to the signs. Undoubtedly you've met such already. Be alert. Be resolute. Maintain an icy resolve. Keep a broad social gulf between you. It is worth the effort.

One final word regarding The Virgin. There are some girls who maintain this condition due to firm moral convictions. They are not necessarily frigid, hostile to men, or in any other way emotionally disturbed. They may very well be among the most well-adjusted, healthy girls you will meet. They are often open, friendly, witty and bright. They are fun to be with. Men have been known to marry these girls. I leave it to you to act accordingly.

The Easy Mark may be found anywhere you happen to be. For the sake of this text the term is meant to be all-inclusive. It refers to the great variety of types who, for one or more reasons, some of which can be delightfully attractive, would like to share their beds with a man Now. The time element is all important with this grouping. Today's Easy Mark may conceivably be unattainable tomorrow.

Does this thought trouble you? It shouldn't. Women are mercurial creatures whose moods fluctuate with no apparent (to the casual male observer) reason. Yet there always is a reason. And a good one, to the woman concerned. She may have suffered a social setback elsewhere and wish to reassure herself that she is still attractive and desirable; she may be lonely, or frightened, or especially insecure and in need of reassurance. She may be competing with another woman, unknown to you. Or she simply may have a powerful urge for sexual fulfillment at the time you meet her. One other possibility comes to mind; she may find your charms irresistible, your sex appeal overwhelming. She may even tell you so. Don't believe it. Just accept your good luck and don't challenge it. Few women are ever *that* overwhelmed by a man. But more about that later.

The important factor in dealing with The Easy Mark is not to rock the boat. She is anxious to introduce you to the mysteries of her bed. Give the girl a chance. She will overlook your boorishness, your lack of grace, your obvious lack of cultural depth and emotional maturity, as well as the fact that your shoes aren't shined, if you let her. But don't go bouncing around all over the landscape collecting telephone numbers. The Easy Mark is not thinking about dinner and a show next Thursday; she's focussing on copulation tonight.

On the other hand, one must not treat The Easy Mark with disdain. She knows what she is doing, may or may not approve of her own actions, objectively speaking, yet may be driven to continue in the path she is travelling. Accord her the same attentiveness you would any other woman. Linger over your late hamburger and coffee in that all-night joint. Don't be too obvious about killing that final drink. Relax. Tension never helped a ballplayer. It simply engenders errors. Don't boot the game-ending out.

I think of The Easy Mark as being only intermittently compulsive about her sexual activities, and then with a certain amount of selectivity. She will not give herself to any man. She reserves the right to change her mind. She will try hard not to reduce herself too much in her own eyes. She recognizes her needs, and wants to do something about them, but with dignity and in keeping with the social standards by which she lives.

There is a variation of The Easy Mark who does not, in fact, cannot, adhere to any standards, external or internal. She, of course, is *The Nymphomaniac.* In medical terminology, nympho-mania is defined as a morbid and uncontrollable sexual desire in a female. The Nympho will sleep with just about anybody, at virtually any time of day or night. Even as I write, I can hear the words of a woman from out of my past:

"I can do it twenty-four hours a day, day and night, with any-one who happens to come along."

Such total lack of discrimination hardly speaks well for the man who accepts her favors. The Nympho uses men the way a furnace does fuel, she burns them up. What are you, a lump of coal?

Go out and build your own fire!

A word about *The Nymphet.* Since "Lolita" hit the bookstalls, there is much talk about nymphets. Everyone is conscious of them. Even The Nymphets are conscious of nymphets. The trou-ble is they try too damned hard. The pouty lips, the doe eyes, the uplift bras, are all very stirring but they are still jail bait. Besides, for how long are you prepared to carry on a conversation about Bobby Darin or someone named Fabian? My advice: leave the little girls to the little boys, and the old men. They can't do better. You can. We hope.

THE FACES

This is not meant to be a treatise on the evils of advertising or the sins of Hollywood. Yet the fact remains that millions of us have been conditioned to want a girl who looks like dear beauti-ful Elizabeth Taylor or that elongated lovely on the billboard.

Those creatures on billboards or in magazine ads have ruined more than one man, and not by direct contact. Rather they pose an ideal which is not only unattainable, it simply doesn't exist. Those ethereal desirables in the ads have little relation to any girl living. And that includes the model who posed for the picture. She might very well have an ugly boil smack in the middle of her chin. But not in the ad. There no blemish is to be seen, magically done away with by means of makeup and a touchup pencil on the negative. In that ad we see no lines of age, concern or character for our girl is every man's dream—perfection!

Of course, in the flesh the model may be slightly different. As a matter of fact, there will be little flesh. She'll probably be bone thin, made up so that she looks like a road company Emmett Kelly, and possessed of all the frailties known to woman. This is not to put down models. Far from it. But the image they project is far removed from reality and a competent lecher will not be blinded by the aura of glamor which surrounds such creatures.

Beauty has created many a problem for man. Stunned by a particular arrangement of nose, eyes, mouth and chin, he ascribes to the owner of said arrangement qualities she may or may not possess. Beautiful girls are very often not the best bed partners. They are, as a matter of fact, frequently disappointing. One of the by-products of beauty is the belief that all things come to the beauty and nothing need be earned. The beauty may, therefore, become a taker, giving little or nothing in return. Sexually speaking, what could be more of a drag!

This spoiled child in a woman's body will inevitably become petulant when denied her own way. She will find means of striking back, of getting even, and what better way than withholding her favors from the beast who is treating her so badly. A friend of mine, during his senior year at college, had the misfortune to meet one of New York's top fashion models. He immediately flipped and vowed to bed her even if he had to marry her. Such a loss of control on the part of a lecher's resolve is, to say the least, dangerous, and many a man has lived a painful existence because of it. It can also be terribly expensive since the cost of rectifying such a wildly impulsive act is astronomical. But back to my friend. Happily, guiding his model friend to the horizontal did not entail marriage. It did, however, entail many weekends together at school and in town. He told me how proud he was on those weekends at school knowing that the best looking girl on campus was with him, the most glamorous girl on campus was with him, the girl most every other man wanted to seduce was with him. When questioned about her sexual prowess he would merely smile enigmatically, since he had never tried to do more than kiss this goddess in high heels.

After several months of heavy dating and outlandish spending, he decided to try and get her drunk and thus accomplish his purpose. It worked like a charm. He never did learn that he could have done the same thing with the same effect on the night he met her. Most everybody along Madison Avenue had. But then he had been blinded by her beauty.

He went with this charmer for nearly a year. During that time she allowed him the freedom of her sleeping bag on only seven occasions. That fellow was a nervous wreck.

"She's not even good," he lamented once. "But I'm hooked on that face."

Moral of the story, as Confucius might say is: "Fish who bite too quick at bait not get meal, but become meal."

Poor fish.

The beauty has an opposite number, the "plain" girl. The experienced lecher will recognize her immediately as a real prize. The lecher deals not in outward appearances so much as with the final results, and the quality of that result. In the plain girl chances are you will strike it rich.

It works roughly like this. Unlike her beautiful sister, the plain girl has seldom been the target for flattering remarks, for overt displays of love and affection, for constant attention. She takes to reading "How To" books on cooking and sewing and she studies Spanish nights at the local Community College. The plain girl learns to live with her loneliness. She doesn't like it but it is a fact of her life.

When someone comes along who removes her from her solitary existence she is flooded with gratitude. Given the chance, she would go far toward displaying her joy and pleasure. Aware, too, that she is far from beautiful, she instinctively recognizes the need on her part to compensate. And, boy, does she compensate! I mean she learns to do things. All things.

In case that's not clear enough, let me put it another way. To most women a steak is just a piece of meat. They seldom go so far as to make it completely inedible, though they stop barely short of that point. But to some kitchen magicians a steak is a challenge, it is color to the artist, words to the writer, the stage to an actor. To such a one a slice of cow becomes an exercise in culinary sleight of hand. She makes the meat better than it is.

See that plain, introspective girl in the corner, the one nobody else at the party pays heed to? Talk to her. Be kind to her. Draw her out. Her feelings run deep. Let her express them. She will. In many ways.

THE SOPHISTICATES

A touchy bunch. Webster's Collegiate defines a sophisticated person as one who is "deprived of original simplicity … highly complicated, refined, … made wise, especially worldly-wise, through experience, disillusionment, or the like." The genuinely sophisti-cated woman is a real prize, much sought after, highly desirable. Hard to get. You gotta be hip. At least as hip as she is.

Very complicated, refined, made worldly-wise, through experience. Such a woman does not offer herself up on a silver platter for the taking. She must be earned. Even before that, she must be recognized. An alarming number of men on the prowl look but they do not see, hear but don't listen, learn but fail to understand.

The genuinely sophisticated woman, as differentiated from the snob, whom we will touch on subsequently, holds herself in high esteem. There is sound reason for such a worthy self-concept. She has permitted herself to experience life in many of its ramifications, and in the experiencing, she has learned some-thing of the world and people, and most important, of herself. Knowing what she is as a human being she is able to make an accurate appraisal of herself, placing herself neither too high nor too low.

This is a person who is no dilletante. Her interest in the vari-ous refinements of life is genuine. She attends theatre or ballet or listens to string quartets because she *enjoys* doing so. She may find pleasure in listening to Sinatra, as well as Elvis, but she is patently able to recognize the differences between the two. She *knows* what it's all about. She may dig Ionesco and Jackson Pollack or she may not; in either case she comprehends her reac-tions, emotional and intellectual, as well as the purposes of the artists. She feels competent to judge their work on merit.

This is not a woman who can be snowed. She will recognize the phony for what he is. The adventurer holds no promise for her. She aims for a deeper exchange with a man, a giving and taking on multiple levels, and she is not prepared to indulge the immature yearnings of callow youth. To get her one must be a man.

It ain't easy.

However, there always is, in the terminology of the advertising community, the reasonable facsimile. There is always something or someone who "looks just like, smells just like, tastes just like," the real thing. There's mink-dyed muskrat, for example, which is muskrat; and compact cars which ride "just like" big ones, but don't, of course; and the stuff that's "just like" the seventy cent spread, but isn't, and on and on and on *ad infinitum ad nauseum.*

Still, for those willing to settle for the reasonable facsimile, here goes. Call her a snob, a dilletante, a phony, it makes little difference. It comes out the same way. She's a *poseur,* something she is not, she's putting on an act, indicating the existence of certain character elements instead of being. She's faking it.

However, since we are less concerned with her character than we are with her flesh, this is of scant consequence. How to recognize her? She approves of everything fashionable, sprinkling her conversation liberally with cultural tidbits meant to impress. Somehow she manages to hit these words harder, making certain they get across. She's the kind of girl who orders Scotch by brand, often some rather obscure name that costs you extra, explaining that she can drink no other brand because they taste so medicinal. Of course, she is served the same bar brand as everyone else and never does know the difference.

She's a cinch. Ripe for the taking. Cater to her. Impress her with your own superficial knowledge. Discuss abstract painting with her. Talk about composition and color design and breaking free of the restrictions of the frame. Throw in a few minutes about college. This is very effective. Also a few choice denigrating remarks about the West Side, the Bronx, Kansas City and Texas serve to heighten your image of a well-rounded phony. She digs you deep and wants to continue the discussion in a more quiet place, which by now you will have suggested.

This does place a certain responsibility on you. You must have a discussion to continue. The failure of the writing alumni of World War II to produce at a continuing high level is always good for an hour or so of pontificating; and you must have a quiet place to take her. Like an apartment. If you flip over this kind of female you may very possibly also be living at home with mama, and may not have an apartment.

Advice: move.

THE MARRIED WOMAN

Do you know what you're getting into? The question is not asked lightly. A married woman on the prowl is a woman with a problem. The core of that problem may or may not be hidden from view but clearly she is a dissatisfied female.

Dissatisfied with her husband, you conclude, vowing smugly to provide what he doesn't. You may have it all wrong. Has it occured to you that a sexual conflict arises in a marriage when a wife, though warm and ardent, may still be sexually cold? Affection, for some women, destroys passion. A married woman committing adultery may bring to the affair complexities the single man hardly desires.

The Biblical injunction which enjoins us against adultery is still in force. It is not unreasonable to question its current validity. There is no question that adultery is no answer to the problems besetting most of us. Yet for some it seems a reasonable solution. There are those for whom an adulterous affair is actually a positive force, making their marriage a much more satisfying condition. A vice-president of a publishing house recounted his forays into adulterous relationships after a monogamous marriage of fifteen years. At forty-five, he met a woman in her early forties who was both attractive and charming.

"I fought against what seemed to be happening," he says. "Yet happen it did. At first I felt guilty, as if I were depriving my wife and family of some precious portion of me. Then my feelings and my thinking began to change. I found I was much more relaxed at home with both my wife and my children. I discovered, too, that I enjoyed making love to my wife now even more than previously. And, to my pleasant surprise, I found out that making love to two passionate women was not beyond my powers."

Undoubtedly such an affair bears sweet fruit for some men. But a single man seeking to establish some kind of a working relationship will find many handicaps attached to an involvement with a married woman. For example: she is seldom available to you when you want her, chances are your arrangement will preclude your phoning her, she'll call you; there are very few places where she will feel safe in appearing with you, and since you can't make love all the time, quick boredom seems inevitable; she may not want you for anything other than your prowess in bed and this may not be quite as flattering as it first appears, most of us preferring a self-concept that makes us out to be more than merely sex machines.

Should none of this matter to you then a married woman may very well bring an added "kick" to your life. Her marital state may evoke in you a satisfaction at cuckolding some other man. One thing is certain, you are very much in the driver's seat with such a lady, and few of us can resist that temptation. One last word of caution: don't get caught. Irate husbands cannot be depended upon to respond to sweet reason.

THE DIVORCEE

Whoopee! is the average reaction of single men to the thought of meeting a divorcee. The thinking goes something like this: A woman used to spending her nights in bed with a man is surely not going to be as difficult to bring to your pad as one who has never been married. Maybe so. However, she might be a tougher nut to crack. Consider this: having just freed herself of one man, a man's she's ostensibly glad to be rid of, why should she take on another, even temporarily?

Still the divorcee does seem to be ripe for plucking. She without doubt is feeling sorry for herself. Some man, the animal, has stolen away her finest years, used her and abused her, cheated her of love and affection and tossed her out into the mainstream of the rat race which she loathes.

Sympathy, in abundant dosages, seems in order. Inundate her with it. Season her food with it. Wrap the flowers you bring her in it. Offer it freely, with warmth. She longs for understanding. So understand her. Give her what she needs. You.

Most women profit from a bad marriage. They take a very realistic view of what has passed and hope not to repeat it. The perceptive and intelligent woman learns from her mistakes. This makes her that much better a companion for the next man in her life. Such a female can make life full and rich in many ways, if given the opportunity. It is this writer's considered opinion that women of experience, having once channeled that experience properly, are fruitful to be with. A man is fortunate to get one. They enhance his days and fill his nights with wonderment.

The Divorcee brings many advantages to a relationship. She is used to cooking for a man, for one thing. She looks upon it as good and natural. Most like fussing for a man and become indignant at the thought of you even doing the dishes afterwards. A word to the wise: offer to wash the dishes. It is an offer invariably refused, at which point you may remove your shoes, hoist your feet onto the coffee table, and sip cognac as you contemplate how good life really is.

Should your apartment need decorating, The Divorcee is obviously experienced and hopefully tasteful. She will be anxious to tour the stores, selecting materials for draperies, offering to "run them off" for you, and pointing out bargains obscured to your masculine eyes. This sort of thing goes on and on, if you permit it, until she feels almost married to you. The connubial couch is the inevitable step.

When you take it remember, the next step, and a short step it is, is to the altar.

She's done it once, she can do it again.

THE LESBIAN

Don't turn up your nose. That cute little number you've been straining to get together with, the one who kisses so expertly and so passionately, yet somehow manages to avoid your grasping paws, she may conceivably be one. Yes, I know she acts and looks fantastically feminine, that she dates men constantly, that she is popular beyond belief. Still, she could be a practicing lesbian.

Most lesbians give no external indication of where their sexual preferences lay. Many of them, in fact, are genuinely fond of masculine company, and some of course will frequently grace a man's bed, though this is not their primary source of sexual pleasure. Many lesbians, as well as male homosexuals, are married and have children. They are called, colloquially, "switch hitters." The possibilities are endless, so don't jump to conclusions.

Some of Hollywood's more glamorous phone numbers are dialed only by women. Many successful women writers seek love from their own kind. And so it goes, in every area of human endeavor.

Few lesbians are as flamboyant as many of their male counterparts. For every "butch" dyke there are ten swishy queens. Nor do women "cruise" in the masculine fashion. By nature more discreet, the lesbian tends to live quietly, generally with a "roommate." They make desirable tenants, desirable neighbors and desirable friends. It is extremely pleasant to have the company of a lovely and personable young girl knowing that neither of you must be "on," but can relax and enjoy each other. So often sex may literally get in the way between a man and a woman, each feeling he must perform in such and such a way, yet not honestly wanting to. Dinner and a few drinks with someone who expects none of this, indeed, desires none of it can prove most rewarding.

I know one young man, friendly with a lovely young lesbian, who always takes her to parties to which he is invited. Both of them are free to operate in whatever manner they wish, utilizing each other as safety valves. It is easy to get out of unwanted invitations by pointing to a companion and claiming a previous engagement.

THE SHY GIRL

You meet her all the time. She is too shy to speak, too withdrawn to look you in the eye, too terrified to stay in one place for very long. She may be cute to look at or mousy and plain. It matters very little. Inside, where it counts, she is neither pretty nor wise nor personable. True or not, it is how she feels. What can one say? Be kind, be generous, be human.

GIRLS AND MONEY

Not prostitutes—they come next. I refer to girls who are handicapped because they have too much money and those who are handicapped because they have too little money. The problem, it seems to me, is identical. No matter what one says or does with these girls, they feel the money is by way of being a blot on their flesh. My advice is that when you run into a girl who feels her father was bestial for becoming rich and forcing her to attend Smith and tour Europe eight times before she was twenty and insists that she buy her clothes at the best shop in town, when you meet that girl agree with her. Money is a curse. Money is evil. Money spoils everything. Agree. Agree. Agree. Get to meet her father as quickly as possible. Explain that you're simply putting her on. Having had to live with it for so many years, he'll understand, probably offer you some good tips on the market. By the way, don't mention it to her.

As to the poor girl who can't stand her father because he *wasn't* rich, well, she has a point there. Give her your sympathy and understanding too. Commisserate with her. A proper choice of parents is, after all, the key to most successful lives.

Remember always the words of the eminent nightclub philosopher, Joe E. Lewis, who said: "I've been rich and I've been poor. And, believe me, rich is better."

THE PROSTITUTE

Commercial romance, while it may serve a definite purpose under certain proscribed circumstances, is a distorted human relationship. It does not concern itself with the paramount value, the value of a human being. It ignores all other values, such as the importance of community and work. The hooker lacks all these, traditionally, and is irresponsible, unsettled, vain and lazy, to say the least.

There is one other thing she is not—and that is oversexed.

According to the law of ancient Rome, a prostitute was a woman who placed herself on the market *passim et sine delectu,* everywhere and without pleasure. What a mature and human concept that is!

There seem to be three general groupings of men who regularly utilize the services of prostitutes:

1) Adolescents, who learn their sexual "reading and writing" from them.
2) Neurotics, who though apparently grownup, act out of fear which makes them reluctant to enter upon a normal sexual or social relationship.
3) The man in the Street, the primitive type who will never reach sexual maturity. The other side of this coin may be the "overly sophisticated man" who is busy grasping at only fleeting relationships, taking what pleasure he can from call girls.

These, then, are the girls. You may say that there are types which are not covered. Perhaps. But I believe they fall mainly into these broad categories. Surely there is sufficient variety here to allow any man to pick and choose, taking his pleasure where he may. Have you made your choice? The next step is to find her ...

CHAPTER THREE

WHERE THE GIRLS ARE ...

ONE of the tragedies of our civilized time is the difficulty some men have in meeting women, and vice versa. The forms by which we live, externally, at least, are rooted in the social mores of another age. They have little to do with this jet-propelled time of ours, yet most of us subscribe to them in part, if not in whole.

The result, of course, is a multitude of lonely people. On any given night young people are forced to sit home bemoaning a fate which dictates they must sit home, though each can be certain that somewhere close by also sits a member of the opposite sex who would be more than willing to give freely of his time, and more. The trick, then, is to bring them together with a minimum of pain.

An intelligent, thoughtful approach to the problem will solve it for the individual. As a matter of fact, many a buck has been turned by guys who have been able to apply business principles to social shortcomings, thus creating artificial social situations which bring people together. Social clubs, resorts, dances, cruises, ski trips, and the like all come under this category to varying degrees. The trick is to find those activities which fit your personality, which do not strain you emotionally, which do not make it increasingly difficult for you to socialize but the reverse. Custom dictates that the man be the aggressor, and for some that is a terrifying thought. So choose those social environments that give you the best of it. A resort with organized activities, that thrusts people together forcing them to communicate at some level may be the answer for you.

For the more outgoing type of personality, the field is unlimited. He simply swings with the action. Girls are everywhere asking, nay, begging to be accosted, romanced and talked into bed. So, here's where the girls are.

I'D LIKE YOU TO MEET ...

The personal introduction is unquestionably the ideal way to meet. It eliminates that awkward first minute or two when neither party is quite certain of his own name or what the hell he's doing there. It also provides a common and safe area to discuss, namely the people who made the introduction.

"Aren't they nice to arrange this meeting?" you might say in a burst of creative energy.

"Oh, yes, very nice," she's bound to agree.

"I count them as real friends."

"Real friends."

"I mean, that's what friendship is."

"Oh, yes."

"Well ... heart, I always say, that's what they've got plenty of."

"You said it. You really said it."

And you did. You really did. This sort of inane conversation has many advantages. It permits you both to get over the initial emotional and verbal stutters without anybody missing anything. It also uncovers areas of common interest, for example:

"Heart," you might continue. "That reminds me of the number in that show, 'Damn Yankees.' Did you see that show?"

"Did I see that show? Did I see it? Are you kidding? Did I see it?"

"Did you?"

"Why I've got theatre in my blood. The only thing is, I don't like baseball."

Immediately you have open to you two areas of conversation, theatre and baseball. The fact that she dislikes the latter has little to do with anything. Obviously she doesn't understand the game. Explain. Explain.

In the continuing search for feminine companionship the lecher will do nothing to discourage the activities of his friends' wives. Wives are challenged by a walking, talking, breathing bachelor much in the same way a bull is by a *torero*. Each is determined to upset the status quo. And understandably so. A bachelor who looks and acts less than miserable is a constant reminder to a husband of another kind of life, a kind of life the wife thinks best forgotten. She sets about removing the spurs to memory.

Let her. The fact that the young women she introduces you to are hell-bent for marriage while you are just hell-bent makes little difference. You must assume that almost every unattached female is seeking to become attached. Their goals, and the routes they follow, must be switched onto paths you choose to follow. As in judo, use their strength against them. Remember that a woman heading toward marriage is also heading toward bed. Also, remember that a body in motion tends to remain in motion. See to it.

Arranged dates very often don't work out. So what! Next time will be better. Encourage the activity. A beneficial by-product of the amateur matchmaker's activity is that you generally get a free, home-cooked meal, something no bachelor in his right mind can afford to overlook. I have spent too many dinner hours in too many ham-and-eggeries with my face buried in the evening edition of a newspaper not to perk up at even the most casual, "Oh, you must come to dinner sometime."

"When?" I always reply eagerly, thus trapping the merely polite.

From this you can readily deduce how vital it is that you cultivate married couples, especially the wives. Husbands seldom will introduce you to gals. Their attitude is that you are a free bird gallivanting about and they will do nothing to help. But the wives, when you meet them at the opening of an art gallery, are always measuring young men in terms of their friends. Make her happy. Let her help you get what you want.

Personally, I'm very big for dinner parties, as must be evident at this point. Not only do they take good care of the inner man, but they make no added social demands upon you in case the female in question turns out to be an absolute third-rater. It isn't necessary to take her anyplace afterwards, except home, and that can be made into a rather speedy, painless operation.

Cocktails present a somewhat different problem. You are *expected* to feed the young lady after each of you has consumed an appropriate number of drinks. If, however, the *raison d'être* for your presence is more than you can humanly bear then you may suddenly remember that your mother in Brooklyn wants you to help move the furniture or perhaps your employer expects you to discuss the new season's sales campaign. Almost any excuse will do since no one will believe it anyway. They will simply shrug internally and wonder what's wrong with the girl. I have one friend who, whenever he's invited for cocktails, arranges with someone to phone him within an hour of his arrival. Someone in his family is always having heart attacks, which are never fatal. His Uncle Fred has had seven such attacks within a two month period, according to my friend, though Uncle Fred is one of those physical fitness nuts who can still be seen running around Central Park in his underwear each dawn.

Personally, I find the introductions made by wives of friends to have proved more fruitful than those made by girls some friend may be dating. Somehow these fall short of expectations. It is definitely a mistake to suppose that because Harry has found himself a prize that all her friends will also be winners. It may happen that way, but don't hold your breath. Single girls, though they may aggressively deny it, cannot help but look on any unmarried male as a prime prospect ... for themselves. This being true, they are less than anxious to give anything away.

However, this rap can be beaten if you have faith in your buddy. Can you trust him to recommend the top quality among the friends of his friend? If you can, then you are in reasonably good shape. Plunge ahead with confidence.

Regardless of how highly recommended the lady comes, however, you and she may not make it. One can match two people quality for quality, interest for interest, taste for taste, and still nothing will happen. Chemistry is the 'X' factor, the unknown quantity. If you're lucky it will be there often and ordinary relationships will take on a magical aura. If it's not, then just put your head down and scramble for yardage.

It's a tough game.

THE BLIND DATE

Sometime it's better if you are!

That's the chance you take. When you reach blindfolded into the grab bag you may come up with a worthy prize or a joker. It's all a matter of chance.

Frankly, I enjoy blind dates. There's a kind of added excitement to not knowing anything at all about a girl. Even if she turns out to be not your type physically the excitement lingers on. Nothing is more fundamentally rewarding than discovering what another human being is all about. On a blind date, that's all there is to do.

We must differentiate between meeting someone at a friends' home for dinner or drinks, or a double date, and the blind date in the purest sense. I'm talking about that phone meeting in which you must identify each other, similar to the following:

"Well, I'm tall, and handsome, I've been told, ha, ha, ha, and I have a thick, shock of black wavy hair. Matter of fact I've been told I ought to be doing those TV hair commercials. You know the ones. I'll be wearing a black silk imported Italian suit, blue striped shirt with a spread collar and a black knit silk tie. And, oh, yes, I haven't a chance to get home yet so I may have a slight beard … !"

And she says, trying not to be ill, but desperate to get out of her apartment for a few hours: "Well, I don't agree with my friends who tell me that I'm beautiful. Pretty. Yes, pretty is more what I am. Anyway, ha, ha, ha, it isn't for me to judge, is it? I'll be wearing a crazy magenta sheath with a plunging neckline which shows off my … oops, well, see for yourself, I always say."

Such a beginning presages an interesting evening. Not necessarily satisfying, but interesting.

No matter how the blind date comes about, if you've committed yourself to it, be brave. Don't get drunk before you call for her. One or two martinis with which to fortify yourself for the ordeal is acceptable behavior. But to come staggering in ready to pass out on her couch just isn't chic.

Another thing. Most girls frown on strange men barging into their apartments seeking to demonstrate their virility at once. It tends to leave a bad impression. Lechery is one thing, but always with dignity. Wait till after dinner.

I would suggest you approach a blind date with a mental list of possible areas of conversation. Blind dates often have a quieting affect on the most garrulous of men. Nothing can be more stultifying than to spend a silent evening with a total stranger smiling uncomfortably at each other, waiting till it's time to go home. Such an experience can set your social life back by many light years. And it can have an unspeakable effect on some fragile female.

A positive approach to blind dating seems indicated all along the line. Plan the evening completely, with alternates, of course, should the lady's taste not match your own. Decide which restaurants are within reach of your pocket, and your taste. You might allow her the choice of rejecting sea food, and perhaps she had Italian the night before. But you select the eating place, you decide where you will have drinks, you choose the club you want to go to. Decisiveness on a blind date is vital. It will ease both of you over the rough spots since, be assured, she does not want to be concerned with making decisions.

Now where did I put that girl's number ...?

VACATIONS

Vacations are either an absolute drag or a mad, mad ball. Somehow there is no middle ground. This being the fact, it is worth spending time and energy in selecting and planning a vacation, be it weekend, two weeks or a more extended affair, carefully and with intelligence.

To begin, take a good look at yourself. Not in the mirror, stupid, inside yourself where it matters. Are you the kind of man who can barge right up to a girl who looks good to you and make conversation without batting an eyelid; or are you the retiring sort who needs not only an introduction but a clearly defined plan of activity? It makes a difference in choosing a place to go.

The brasher types can go anywhere, and if they don't feel at home, you'd never know the difference. They can swing their weight around oblivious to what anyone else wants to think. Many times such a self-centered fellow is losing ground rapidly with some girl, yet is unaware of the fact. As she toddles off with that quieter chap, he merely shrugs and looks for another target. Few of us are that way. Fortunately, I might add.

For those who are really shy it is best to choose a place that boasts a well-organized social program. Resort hotels fit this description best. There are organized athletics, dancing classes, water skiing and so on. These and more, give one the opportunity to meet and talk to girls under the most favorable circumstances. An afternoon of water skiing, for example, may provide conversational fodder for that entire evening. And the next day you can water ski again. It's rather a self-perpetuating activity.

I'm a firm believer in dance classes. First of all, they help you to dance better, and this is a definite social asset. Girls like to dance. Girls like to dance with men. Men get to hold girls when they dance, hold them close. Holding girls close is good. Holding girls close gives rise to other social activities. Dance, boy, dance.

Such well-organized resorts draw a variety of types, of both sexes. The more expensive places have a strong economic base in their clientele: those who have money and those who want it. To the lecher such thoughts are merely diversionary, and he will adjust easily to the situation, shifting with the winds, you might say.

Clothes play a major part in your vacation and evenings are generally "dress" affairs. The dolls doll up and expect you to do likewise. To defy them in this area is to court absolute social disaster.

Note: privacy is hard to come by at such resorts. Most rooms contain two or more men or women, often strangers to each other. It takes much planning and smooth operating to get a girl alone.

Beach resorts, especially those with an arty flavor such as Fire Island and Provincetown, offer an entirely different milieu. Here informality is the watchword. Grouping for the season is accepted behavior. Four or five fellows will take a house together, with the girls doing likewise. Parties are constant and open to virtually everyone. Weekends at Fire Island are just one long round of parties, as people roam about, glasses in hand, listening for the sound of other Islanders at play. Partying sounds draw more party-goers and one need merely turn around and talk to whoever is there. After a few such parties on a given evening, one forgets all about dinner and may well fall into a bed somewhere. Any bed. Anywhere. With anyone. Informality, as I pointed out earlier, is the watchword.

The beach almost anywhere, however, offers opportunities galore for meeting girls. Obviously, it presents one with an outstanding chance to really judge the material. The bikini leaves nothing much to the imagination. Blanket hopping is an accepted form of behavior and a simple, "Hello," will generally get you an invitation to be seated. At four-thirty or so, people begin thinking about cocktails. By five, the beach starts to empty, and another round of partying has begun. This is a situation which has great appeal to men who are quick on their feet, have unlimited powers of recuperation, and are concerned primarily with quantity not quality.

Even such wide-open societies make certain demands. To begin, there is something about the combination of surf, sand and sun that turns on the Intellectual-Cultural circuit in people. Perhaps it is a form of compensation for the obvious physicality of the life they lead. In any case, it's open season on any subject and you are expected to contribute. A working knowledge of Freud, Jung, Adler, et al, is a must. You should be able to provide a quick analysis of anyone's problems on the spot. Accuracy is less important than glibness. A glance at a few back issues of *Time Magazine* should be more than enough preparation.

Some general information: start dieting no later than March 1st, flat bellies still being much in vogue; read a few current best-sellers so you can sound off about how much you dislike them. (Knock the successful is a good rule to follow at all resorts.) *Don't,* repeat, don't, point out the most successful lechers on the beach, it gives the lady something to consider to your own detriment; do put down lechery in general, thus implying in your most subtle manner that your interest goes beyond the mere physical; don't overdo the previous suggestion, some girls just want the action.

Like so many other things in life, the key to a successful vacation is motivation. I sincerely believe it to be a serious mistake to make the prime purpose of a vacation the meeting and bedding of females. It won't always happen, in which case your vacation is a dismal bust. Rather go away with a sound reason. You like to swim, or play tennis, or simply because you need a rest. Frankly, too much social pressure internally will push you right on your face. Relax. Enjoy yourself. Don't push too hard. It's an attitude most men don't have on vacation, so that when they do women are so flabbergasted they can't keep their lovely little hands to themselves. Play it cool, man.

YOUR JOB

This is a touchy area. Many schools of thought exist as to the advisability of playing where you eat. There are those dead set against it, pointing out that working in such close proximity to someone whom you have been dallying with is not in the best of taste. What is really behind this objection is the sense of guilt which many of our sex feel over what they have done. They look upon their little forays as betrayals of womanhood in the best bourgeois tradition. We have only pity for them.

A swinging chick is a swinging chick, even if she does your typing. What is required is a firm control of life, *your* life. In the office you maintain, and see that she does too, a strong sense of business decorum. It isn't as difficult as it may appear. Is she working for you or are you working for her? What it really gets down to is this, you must be sure that she has a thorough and accurate picture of your relationship. Too often a succumbing female creates a situation which doesn't exist. When becoming involved with a fellow worker you must prevent this from happening.

Should you work for a company which forbids employees to date each other, then by all means date anyone you want. This provides built-in security against being annoyed during the day by a clinging female. With her job at stake, she will act in a decent and upright manner. If you are working for such a mid-Victorian firm and do establish a nice, healthy sexual relationship with one of the office girls, play it smart. It's perfectly all right to sleep together, to breakfast together, even to travel to work together (although I tend to frown on the latter activity somewhat), but for God's sake, don't stand around holding hands during a coffee break. Gauche!

One thing about meeting women at your job, it is simple. It takes no effort to talk to one of your choosing, and subjects for conversation are always near at hand. And for you shy chaps, no girl in her right mind is about to turn down a free lunch. Feel confident about operating in this area. Most girls look upon their jobs as simply another opportunity to meet eligible men: be equally sneaky. Girls change jobs quite often for no other reason but that the men don't suit them. Take them out. Wine them and dine them. Make much of them. Permit them to succumb to you. It will save them the employment agency fee.

TRAVELLING

The travelling man has never had it so good. Economy flights, cruises, and other transportation advances have made it possible for the single, working girl to be able to afford to travel abroad. She flies or floats out of reality into the fantasy world of the Caribbean or Europe leaving responsibility behind her. She wants to have a good time. Often she throws caution wherever it is one throws caution. It seems only fitting that a healthy young male step in and fill the ensuing void.

Again a word of caution about motivation. To invest the time and money required for most trips abroad with a view toward giving free rein to your reproductive urges is to commit a form of social Hari-kari. Europe, for example, offers so much more than its beds. It is a world far different than our own and to explore it with curiosity and vigor guarantees immense rewards. To share these treasures with a warm and willing companion will enhance every experience. If nothing else, your new cosmopolitan image will do wonders to your relationships with impressionable females.

I recommend travelling alone. This takes courage, but it offers much more. It gives you the freedom to come and go as you like. If you choose to remain in a particular city longer than planned you must account to no one. If you want to study the architectural wonders of Paris you needn't feel guilty about a friend to whom all buildings look alike.

As a matter of fact, being able to pursue your primary interests in such a manner will inevitably lead you to girls with similar tastes. The gargoyles of Notre Dame have opened many a conversation which later resulted in sharing a jug of wine, some French bread and a French bed. The rewards of culture are manifold.

It's a good idea when travelling to come prepared with phone numbers and addresses supplied by your friends, just in case. Meeting the native population promises to widen your social horizons, notably if some of them are female and available. A poor but cleancut American lad alone on a strange continent might well require a native guide. Such an association could conceivably lead to a strong bond being established between you, a bond difficult to sever, a bond that makes demands, demands that somehow must be satisfied. Language barrier or no, I'm certain that between you you'll figure out something, the sort of thing will inevitably lead to a lessening of international, not to mention personal, tensions.

While travelling one has certain decided advantages in making new friends. No matter how well one may speak the language of the country you're in, it may be conveniently forgotten if doing so aids in furthering a relationship. It is the wise man who will get lost whenever he spots an attractive girl. Ask for help. Throw yourself upon her mercy. Then, having accepted her good offices, you must repay her somehow. Dinner? A drink? A left-bank club?

Who needs Berlitz?

Meeting a native of the country you happen to be in promises to improve your trip in many ways. It gives you an opportunity to go to the places your new friend normally patronizes, keeping you away from the usual overpriced tourist traps. Back home are one hundred and eighty-five million Americans. Believe me, they'll still be here when you get back, complete with drive-in movies, striped tooth paste and push-button cans. Europe can be a fascinating world, a different world which reaches back much further than our own. The result is the people look at life somewhat differently, shaped by different traditions and different values. Enjoy them and what they have to offer.

Especially the girls.

PARTIES

Some people believe in vitamins. Others vegetables. I believe in parties.

Parties are great for a male on the prowl since it gives him the rare opportunity to operate on two levels—present and future. A competent male roams freely collecting telephone numbers for future reference, all the while keeping an eye peeled for present action. I call these, "recruiting parites." All this must be done of course with no offense to anyone, otherwise it's no contest. It's simple enough to antagonize the women whom you store away as a squirrel stores nuts for future emergencies, but it does show a certain lack of class.

The big thing about parties is the assumption you may accurately draw. Namely: *she* is there to meet a man. That rule of thumb holds true for whoever you happen to be eyeing lasciviously. Matter of fact, she hopes you are. That's why she's wearing that hip-hugging black with the neckline down to here. She means for you to look, so look. But speak not of what you see, if speak you must. Sophistication demands that you not stoop to such levels. Want to impress her? Tell her how much you love that bump on the bridge of her nose. She's been considering a nose job for years now, you may be assured. Talk her out of it. Tell her how weary you are of faces that look just like other faces. Find the fault and tell her it's a virtue. She'll want to believe you even if she doesn't. Most important, she'll listen.

Parties are prime places for the man seeking a quickie. It takes a certain amount of perception and a realistic approach to life. Most men delude themselves about this. They talk a good game but fumble the ball every time. The practiced lecher has his radar switched on even as he joins a party. He knows precisely what he is seeking. His is a no nonsense approach with only one thing in mind. Trusting his senses, his instincts, he trusts those in women also. He reasons that he is sending out silent signals and that they will be received by his female opposite number. Boing! There she is, seated demurely against the wall, a half smile on her sweet face. She meets his glance openly. She has nothing to hide. Hide! She'd like to shout it to the world. He moves in quickly. He *knows*.

The less skilled practitioner would never choose this girl. Perhaps she isn't pretty enough for him. Nor is she chic enough. Nor does she possess the bloated mammary glands thought to indicate something or other. She appears much too mild-mannered to even consider as an Easy Mark, yet that is exactly what she is. The man interested in quality of performance recognizes a kindred soul. This firefly is sending out his signal. Signal received. Am coming in for a landing.

Welcome aboard.

Once you have zeroed in on a likely prospect at a party, make your exit quickly, chick in hand. Take her to dinner. Or a quiet, dimly lit saloon. Or feed her hamburgers, if necessary. But get her alone. Crowds can do you no good now. Force her to focus on you. No sense letting her draw comparisons with some other character. You might come out second in a two horse race.

The best parties are attended by only two people—a man and a girl.

BARS

I also believe in bars. Any experienced hunter in the wilds of a city will agree. Being in a bar is like hunting ducks from a blind; you simply have to sit and wait. When the duck you want flaps into view, let 'er have both barrels.

Now in every saloon you are going to find a girl (or girls) sitting by herself sipping a drink and staring sightlessly into space. You are going to decide that this girl and you were mated by fate. You amble over, perch on the adjoining stool, show her your teeth, and introduce yourself.

"I don't know you," this girl is going to say, in her most cutting manner, and loudly, too. "I don't have anything to do with anyone I don't know. We haven't been introduced and I hope we never are. Go away."

Don't argue with this one. Just tuck your tail between your legs and run. That's a very bad girl. She's not for you. Believe me. You must learn to quit while you're bleeding only a little bit. I have known men who have come out of an evening trying to scale the battlements surrounding such a creature cut to ribbons, their manhood in tatters, defeated, deflated, destroyed. Pull back. Move out. Tell yourself it's not a defeat, that you're only shortening your lines of communication. Find yourself another piece of fluff.

I always assume that every unattached female in a saloon is there to meet me, company described above excepted, else why would she be there? I believe that very few women, singly or in groups, enter bars primarily because they want a drink. They are lonely. They are distraught. They are frantic. Desperate. Panicky. But they're not thirsty.

With this thought to bolster one's confidence, barge right in on anybody you want. Don't be afraid. Prepare a few alternate lines of attack, in case she decides to be tricky:

"I noticed you sitting here by yourself."

Or,

"What's that peculiar concoction you're drinking?"

Or,

"What's a nice girl like you doing in a place like this?"

Though none of the above are particularly original, especially that last one, they do give you some indication what line of thought to follow. It's entirely possible, of course, that you can come up with something much better. If you know the bartender well, and it appears he knows her, get him to introduce you. Ask him out loud. It's a good gambit.

There are certain indications of a girl's attitude about the things that *matter* that may be gleaned from her drinking habits, to wit: drinkers of rye and ginger ale are so steeped in middle-class virtue as to be almost completely lost; whisky sour people are sippers and have no intention of getting too jolly; the straight Scotch girl bears watching; that Sherry drinker may possibly be a wino. But it is the martini girl on whom you should rivet your attention, particularly if it is no later than four in the afternoon. To state the case without equivocation, nobody really *enjoys* martinis. That isn't why people drink them. A lone woman in a bar drinking one before six is,

a) striking a pose of sophistication, a pose that you in your sophistication can penetrate at a glance, and,

b) she's going to get potted.

Help her along. If she's still standing by eight o'clock the thought of dinner will undoubtedly sicken her. There is only one thing to do—take her home. Yours or hers.

Some bars are friendlier bars than other bars. Each city has them. The pretty girls all flock to them giggling and happy and simply dying to have dinner with some smooth young guy. Find your friendly bar, patronize it. Make friends. It will be good for you.

You don't like to drink …?

Then learn!

SPORTS

Action begets action, is another of my homilies guaranteed to pay off. I'm for anything that gets the blood coursing through your veins and her veins at a pace somewhat in excess of Old Man River's. Even in this sedentary world of ours a woman likes to believe that the man she gives herself to has at least a couple or three muscles in his body that aren't atrophied. Prove it to her.

Another thing to consider about sports is the manner in which they draw women. Originally, women were attracted to sports because that was where the men were. Now many areas of athletic endeavor are inundated with females. Skiing, for instance.

Women are strewn all over ski slopes in dire need of masculine assistance. It is incumbent upon you to provide it. To start, teaching a girl to ski can be fun. It can be exceedingly difficult to get a fallen girl back on her skis. It involves many intricate maneuvers of arms and bodies. People sometimes fall on people. Still, it's a way of passing the time.

And the girls look wonderful in those stretch pants they wear. Girl watching societies have come into being on the best slopes. There are men who make every ski weekend during the season simply to watch the girls in their ski pants. Try it and see. Back at the ski lodge it is rather easy to get acquainted with that trim number in the blue outfit. You have a common interest to discuss—skiing, I mean. And those nights can get awfully cold. On a given weekend you'll meet a number of attractive girls, girls who are not afraid to go places and do things. It makes life much more interesting that way. And in addition to everything else, you will unquestionably have a wonderful time skiing.

Tennis is great for meeting people, girl people. Everybody looks very athletic in those white things, which adds a sort of overlay of purity to the proceedings that is not without a certain charm. Tennis is excellent exercise, will help you work off that spare tire, and if you are smart enough to smack a few balls onto the next court where those cute girls are playing, you may have company that evening.

A friend of mine has never set foot on a tennis court in his life, but he takes himself to the public courts in New York's Central Park each Sunday, dressed in shorts and sneakers and carrying his racket. He parks himself on the grass and strikes up conversations with girls of his choosing who are waiting for their turn at the courts. When the girl he has selected finishes her game he invites her for coffee. This elicits the following exchange, more or less.

"That's very nice of you. But you haven't played yet," she will say.

He, with a shrug, replies, "Well, it won't kill me to miss one day."

BONNIE GOLIGHTLY & JONATHAN STARR

Now do you fully grasp the subtleties of this approach? It borders genius. Only another tennis player can wholly comprehend the sacrifice entailed in giving up a game on a public court, where sometimes a player must wait for three or four hours for his turn. To pass up a game for a mere girl is akin to a declaration of love everlasting. It moves such a skilled operator far along the road he desires to travel.

Boating is a make-out sport. Taking a girl aboard someone else's boat is all right, though entailing certain obvious risks. If you have your own boat, or rent one (a very smooth move), you are in very good shape. Implicit in boating are any number of factors that work in your favor. Owning and operating a boat is expensive. Rich men are automatically more attractive than the other kind. Boating is like the America Cup competition, almost. There's the flags flying and the wind blowing through her hair and Jackie and the President watching it all. It's almost like a cigarette commercial. And if your boat sleeps two ... well!

Swimming is without par for the female oriented male. In the first place, no public activity permits the two of you to wear fewer articles of clothing. And the current fashion in bikinis defies description. Embracing girls—out of pure affection, of course—who wear bikinis is one of the more delightful ways of passing time on a beach. All that sun-heated flesh!

The amazing part of swimming is the possibilities it presents for fleshy pursuits while dunking the body. Much contact is permitted while in the surf that might be frowned on under drier conditions. Teaching a delicate lass the art of paddling about in the waves offers many fine chances to the enterprising for solidifying a friendship, and puts the young lady forever in your debt.

And so it goes! Skating, bowling, ping pong, water skiing, golf, are but a few of the activities that women enjoy and participate in. A favorite female may, of course, be taken along on those outdoor activities which you especially find pleasurable. Hunting or fishing, for example. Girls may not really care for roughing it to that degree, yet few of them will refuse an invitation to go camping out. It would destroy the image they're trying to project, of being man's best and most rewarding companion. Camping should put a gleam in your eye when you consider the size of those tents (need I advise you against taking along more than one?).

Certain spectator sports are outstanding aids in getting a girl in the mood. Football, for one. An afternoon watching an army of muscle seek to destroy another army of muscle raises the red corpuscle count of just about any girl. A drag from a flash helps also. Afterward, your companion will be warming up. I leave that to you.

The *pièce de résistance* in spectator activity is the race track. It exerts pressures on the ladies that even they aren't aware of. There is the excitement of the races themselves; the thrill of winning or losing money; the highly communicable tension of the crowd; and the gratitude over which she feels toward you for supplying all that cash she is losing. If she wins, look out brother! She'll love you to death.

A warning against girls who play chess well—they are used to thinking at least one move ahead and thus constitute a real and present danger. Avoid them. Unless you can beat them at their own game.

MUSEUMS

Absolutely among the best locations for finding what you're looking for. And the highest quality merchandise, too. Reasons to begin a conversation abound. Any painting or sculpture will do. I find it is best to be rather ignorant, to ask questions, seek explanations. *Get them to talking.* After a while—a leisurely pace is suggested under these circumstances—raise the question of coffee or a drink. Give her the choice. You will learn much, not only from which she chooses, but by her manner. A reluctant, "A Coffee will be fine," is hardly encouraging for the present, while a brisk "I'd love a martini," should evoke a sense of genuine accomplishment in your eye.

In my meandering, I favor the museums of modern art, and similar galleries. This is not to denigrate the girls patronizing the more traditional halls. Far from it. They're generally outstanding examples of their sex. No, it is simply a matter of taste, and I lean toward the devotees of Miro and Klee who seem to possess a heightened sense of their own emancipation.

Zoos offer certain possibilities, I suppose, but I always get the feeling that the animals are peering through those bars with pity in their eyes. I can live without that.

SOCIAL CLUBS

Strictly a bad scene. All the picked-over people of the world are in attendance. One gets a sense of a mass drowning with a silent cry thickening the atmosphere, "Save me! Save me!"

What are you, a life preserver?

PICKUPS

I refer strictly to those meetings that come about in such public places as the streets, the lobbies of movie palaces, train stations, and the like. Pickups are great if you can pull them off. Frankly, the effort is generally not worth the struggle, in my opinion. Most girls are dead set against being so accosted, though occasionally you might come up with a real winner. I've seen some who have.

I am reminded of the old tale of the lecher who prowled the streets asking every girl he met to decorate his mattress. He had his face slapped many times, but every now and then found a funmate.

POLITICS

This is in keeping with my philosophy about a purpose beyond mere socializing. An interest in politics is admirable, patriotic and frequently sexually stimulating. Pretty girls abound in political clubs, neither party being short-changed, I might add. Join your local Democratic or Republican club and get involved in their activities. There will be a job that fits your talents and will bring you into close contact with many sympathetic types.

AMATEUR THEATRICALS

Great hunting ground. If you're a frustrated actor, join some little theatre group. You won't be frustrated long.

As previously indicated, many of us males have difficulties in the initial approach. This is no secret. Millions of people are hard at work trying to make it easier for you. Almost all of them, aside from this writer, are women. Yes, women. They *want* you to come up to them brashly, even cockily, though tastefully, and make leading remarks. Most of them don't care what you say, really, as long as you do.

Let me point out some of the things women do to encourage you. To begin with, they undergo the tortures of the damned in an effort to appear attractive, enticing, sexy, beautiful, for you. That's right—you! Oh, sure, they take pride in their own appearances but no woman ever struggled into a girdle for her own sake, or spent hours in a beauty salon, or tried on every dress in the shop until she found the one that makes her look irresistible. Those are the obvious moves. Let's look beneath the surface.

Black underwear is a big seller. Ask any lingerie salesman. It's a bull market for lace panties. It ain't because girls necessarily prefer black, but because of what black seems to connote to you, and you, and you. A girl in black underwear is a girl in hope.

At the more obvious level, our lady friends have loads of little tricks to bring us within their orbits. For example, they wear jewelry designed to evoke comment, pins that spell out their names (in case they forget it, I suppose), or sport provocative slogans like "Why fight it?" They carry controversial books, displaying the titles prominently, they jingle charm bracelets, they spill their drinks, they lose matches, let their watches run down, and they still drop handkerchiefs. You may assume these acts are deliberate on their part and permit her the luxury of having her plans work successfully.

Say hello. She'll love you for it.

CHAPTER FOUR

WHAT TO DO ABOUT IT ...

HAVING DECIDED what kind of women you'd like to meet, and knowing where to find them, you have only to insure success in your venture. Life being the uncertain thing it is, this is easier said than done. Very often one *believes* he is doing things properly, yet the results are far from happy. This brings us back to a subject touched on briefly earlier—attitude.

Attitude is much more than simply striking a pose or mouthing a platitude. It involves *being* a certain kind of human being. This may neccesitate a complete revamping of your outlook. Frightening? Perhaps. But it may be the shortest route to social success. To begin, women like men. Not a startling statement until we explore its meaning.

Men are not only those males who have achieved their full physical growth. There is much more. A mental growth and an emotional one. Women desire maturity in a man. This does not refer to years so much as it does to outlook. A woman feels entitled to a lover who is equipped to cope with the problems that will arise in his *life*. She does not expect her man to step into the ring with Sonny Liston, that's not his cup of tea; she does not expect him to wrestle alligators or kill grizzly bears with a sling shot. But she does expect—and she has a right to—that he is capable of slaying the dragons of his own place and time.

A Man is capable of taking charge of a situation, not brusquely and with hostility, but gently and with firmness. He will face the natural enemies of his kind—cab drivers and waiters—with strength and fortitude. He will not be subservient to those who serve him. Nor will he bully them. He will have learned how to say no when he doesn't choose to do something or go somewhere. Too often men allow themselves to be towed about contrary to their own desire. As a corollary, he will have clearly defined tastes in the various areas of life—in food, in restaurants, in entertainment, in sports, in dress, in music, in women. He will have opinions. He will make judgments. He will seek to shape life to his own designs rather than being tossed about by it.

However, since few of us are such paragons, we must compensate, learn to fake it, if you will. Learn to simulate the real thing. Let us assume that you have invited a young thing who has stimulated your imagination up to your apartment for dinner. You are not a chef *par excellence* by any means, nor are you a wine steward. What to do? The answer is obvious. Were you faced with the same problem while in college or in the work area you would know what to do … you would learn. The same thing applies here. Learn.

It is important to begin properly. Most girls having been lured to a male's apartment expect to be plied with 9 to 1 martinis, stuffed with steak, given five or ten minutes respite then assaulted carnally. Don't do it. Throw her off stride.

Start with an aperitif. At once visions of Paris or Madrid will float before her eyes. A vermouth cassis should at once slow her heartbeat, calm her nerves, pique her appetite. After all, you did invite her for dinner. You might give her a choice in this matter, perhaps Byrrh, or Pernod, or if she prefers bitters, the Italian Campari.

While you are sipping your aperitif, discussing Leonard Bernstein's contributions to the world of music, you might well serve the *antipasto* rather than the standard onion soup and cream cheese mix with wheat thins. If you really want to be exotic you might make up a small salad of greens with salami and provolone. This is guaranteed to make important points for you.

The key to such an evening is pace, tempo. Let events take their natural course, set their own rhythm. Force nothing. Let sexuality arise in counterpoint to normal social behavior. Have a second aperitif. But no more.

Now to the meal. Stay away from the commonplace. How about a Clam Broth Bellevue? Simple to make, this is an inspiring seafood classic. As she sips this she will see you in a new light, and you will take on dimensions in her eyes you never before possessed.

I would stay with the seafood theme. It possesses a glamor meat somehow does not project. Try fried oysters with sesame. Exotic, yet satisfying, it has the appeal of the familiar with the excitement of the new. A good Rhine wine, or perhaps a Chablis, to go with the oysters. You have moved a large step forward.

This is all offered by candlelight. Corny? Perhaps, but it still works wonders, dressing up the occasion. You personally should add to the total picture. A tie and jacket are not necessary, but they tend to help. If you prefer not to dress that formally, then surely be neat and suitably casual.

Finish off with coffee. Demi-tasse or regular. If desert you must have, then a wedge of camembert will do. Then it is time for some soft music, gentle conversation, and a good brandy.

Voila! It is done.

All of this should take place against the appropriate background. I assume you live alone. Roommates are perfectly all right for school boys, but when a grown man has one of those a woman has a right to wonder what manner of man is this. A poor one, at least, and money matters should never interfere with business. I would sacrifice a chic neighborhood or a more fashionable building in favor of a lower rental if it meant solitude. The thought of another man suddenly barging in is enough to give any girl the willies.

I believe the apartment is in many ways one of man's most important attributes. Let's explore it in some detail. In what part of town should you live? Naturally, you would prefer living in a section convenient to your job. But don't let this consideration be foremost in your mind when choosing a place to live. Ten minutes extra on a bus won't kill you while a glamorous or exotic location may very well do you much good.

The type of building you select is vital. New buildings have a built-in acceptance, of course, newness somehow being linked with quality. Personally, I lean toward the older but somewhat unique type of dwelling. The old brownstones in New York with their high ceilings, shuttered bay windows and working marble-faced fireplaces promise immeasurably more than the contemporary boxes being erected willy-nilly around town. In the day of the elevator, a walkup takes on a certain quaintness, and quaintness works for you.

Patios and gardens are tremendous assets. Dinner on a patio enhances the dinner, the apartment and, mainly, you. I would not be concerned with lavish fronts or entrance foyers in a building, but I make certain that any building I contemplated moving into was well-kept and clean. Girls notice things like that and are reluctant to give freely of themselves in circumstances that make them feel "icky," as they put it.

When it comes to decorating an apartment, I'm a do-it-yourself man. That is, I'd want to select every item by myself. In certain areas I recognize my need for assistance. For example, if you have faulty color perception get someone to help you. Some girls are only too happy to contribute their time and energy to such endeavors. It gives them a feeling of being wanted.

Cost needn't be a major deterrent to furnishing your own place. Careful shopping will uncover genuine bargains in the furniture field. Curb the tendency to buy cheap modern, than which nothing is more garish, or unpainted horrors. Despite all efforts to disguise the latter they still look like unpainted horrors painted. Try this idea for size. In every city there are numerous shops that sell old used furniture quite inexpensively. A marble-topped Victorian chest can be turned into a decorator's piece. Take it down to the natural wood with stain remover and sand-paper, then finish it with a few coats of wax or some lemon oil. The rich oak or walnut will look better as time passes.

Simplicity is the key to furnishing well and inexpensively. A single Chinese-type lamp purchased for $11 in a department store, looks like the real thing in the proper setting. And I am writing this on a desk made of old sewing machine legs, freshly painted, and a flush door. Canvas and wood director's chair provide inexpensive seating while a cut down dining table makes for a practical and attractive coffee table. So it goes. A travel poster on one wall, a unique and colorful square of fabric from Pakistan in a frame on another, provide attractive hangings.

When furnishing it is wise to remember that you are better off doing without something than buying a piece you are not genuinely fond of. Such things wear on your nerves and grow uglier with the passage of time. Take your time. It will save you money and distress.

Hi-fi seems to be *de rigeur* with the modern male. Without it he seems lost. I'm all for it, as well as for stereo, if you can manage to keep in mind that they are for listening to not for talking about. I get bored hearing people spout off about tuners and woofers and what the hell have you. I'm certain girls feel likewise. If a hi-fi or stereo unit are out of reach of your pocketbook you can obtain the same effect—the mollifying of female suspicions and inflaming of female desire—with a good record player. Personally, I'm inclined toward a good FM radio. I simply collect all the program guides and that way can get to listen to just about any kind of music at any time of day. It saves the cost of costantly purchasing new records, or tapes, if that's your kick, and serves me very well. I commend it to you. By all means, have some sort of music. It pulls the entire picture together.

I'm a book man myself. I like them around. They please me and fit in with my image of myself. I suspect most women prefer a man who reads occasionally, and that means something other than the sports pages. I recommend being hip to D. H. Lawrence. I've never known a female (a hip female, that is) who didn't flip over his work. Try leaving an open volume of "Lady Chatterly's Lover" on the mantel.

I like parties, as I've said. I like attending them and I like giving them. Giving them can add considerable stature to your public image as a *bon vivant.* A successful party is composed of several compatible ingredients, none particularly difficult to assemble. Clever, witty men and pretty girls, an abundance of liquor and a shortage of chairs. Successful parties are mainly in the vertical. The moment people begin sitting down they tend to remain put. Keep them circulating. And do so yourself.

As host, it is your duty to see that your guests have everything they want. This permits you to talk to all the girls, especially those whom you never met before. Flirt with as many as you like. Collect phone numbers wholesale. After all, it is your party.

If you've been wise you will have invited one girl to serve as your hostess. She will happily do most of the work. It's amazing how girls love to do things like that for a man. It's something in their nature. Then, when the party breaks up, and everyone departs, she will inevitably remain behind to help you clean up. *Don't let her do it!* Fix her a last drink. Insist that she relax on your couch. Relax beside her, after dimming the lights. By now it is rather late. Fate being what it is she lives on the other side of town. Taxis are difficult to find at this time of night. She will see the logic of your position. Possessed of a warm feeling after the successful festivities, she will be more than amenable to any suggestions you may have.

Think of something.

I am a firm believer in enjoying parties, whether they be your own or not. Upon the arrival of every new guest, I suggest you thrust a drink in his hand, at the same time pointing out where the liquor is. After that it is every man for himself. I make it a point to introduce each new arrival to one or two people, but no more. People will seek each other out and those mass name callings are useless and fun-killers.

No less important to the single man than his apartment, and how it looks, are his clothes, and how they make him look. If clothes do not make the man, they surely help make the woman. Each of us has a definite image of, if not how we look, how we'd like to look. The well-dressed male makes a marriage between what he is and what he'd like to be. He dresses in accord with his appearance. Nothing looks sillier than some monstrous wrestler-type in a pair of those pipestem trousers. And men with flabby bellies shouldn't wear low-rise, tight pants; the fat overflows like Niagra Falls.

Take a good look at yourself. All styles may not be for you. Choose those that are. What's right for Cary Grant is not

BONNIE GOLIGHTLY & JONATHAN STARR

necessarily so for Fred Astaire, yet they both dress extremely well. The key to being well-dressed is not necessarily money, in case you didn't know, it is taste. And that comes from within. Good taste really refers to the ability to do the utmost in terms of what you are.

Your budget will, of course, play a part in the clothes you purchase. If it is limited then start out with those items which can double in brass. A navy blue suit can be worn to work, to cocktails, to the theatre. A tweed suit plus a contrasting pair of slacks provides two outfits, since the jacket can serve as a sports coat. Accessories should be purchased in the same manner; a black knit tie goes with just about everything. A pair of black wingtips and a pair of brown loafers will cover you in the shoe department adequately, if your funds are limited.

If money is no problem then the above doesn't apply to you. Simply patronize the best men's shops in town, buy everything your little heart desires, and strut about. Chances are at least fifty-fifty that you will come out looking like a self-conscious peacock. Where can you buy good taste? It's not for sale. But it is available to those who desire it. Look around. What public figures do you admire?

Movie stars, politicians, athletes, executives. If they are well-dressed, then they have one thing in common, they wear only those things which are most flattering to *themselves*. Learn from them. Read the men's magazines, study the ads, decide what suits you and what doesn't. Window shop the *best* shops in town. This means the shops that are *traditionally* top rated, the ones whose styles have stood the test of time. You may not be able to afford their clothes but you will be able to find less expensive versions elsewhere.

Make certain your clothes fit properly.

No matter how expensive or fashionable your garb may be, it comes out second rate if it isn't cut in terms of your figure. This is the advantage of custom made clothing, as every man who has his suits made realizes.

Wear your clothes without strain. Let them become a part of you. After that last look in the mirror, forget about them. There's nothing further you can do. The women will look at you and approve or not, depending on how effective a job you've done.

The way you look is a definite reflection of your own self-concept. Other people recognize this, and women are particularly aware of it. Show them that you think well of yourself.

They will too.

CHAPTER FIVE

SO YOU THINK YOU'RE SEXY ...

BUT DOES anyone else? Mainly women. Anyway, one must point out the essential difference between *being* sexy and *feeling* sexy. The latter had to do only with your desire. The formed has to do with the way women respond to you, the feelings you evoke in them. Most of us feel sexy with some degree of regularity, like every hour on the hour. But evoking the proper response in members of the opposite sex is quite another matter.

The question is, have you got it? If not, is it available? And where can you get some?

You must answer the first question for yourself. If the answer you come up with is in the negative, then I can assure you that the answers to the next pair of queries are affirmative. Definitely. Yes, Clarence, sexiness is available. In great, lush, heaping gobs. And do you know where it is? Right smack inside you. Located loosely somewhere behind your navel. The real question is how to bring it out into the open.

For a starter, you must learn to love women. Not some women, but all women. Then add to this your special tastes in women and you'll find yourself overwhelmed with desire for them. But you must love them in all their many ramifications. You must love all of their separate parts, their strong points, their shortcomings, love them when they please you and love them (through your annoyance) when they give you a hard time.

Look around you at the women you know, at those you pass in the streets. Those you find sexy, don't they carry themselves in a special way, don't they project an intangible pride in self? That's a woman feeling wonderful about being a woman. She is sexy. You must find that same sense of manhood. It matters not at all what you look like or how you're built. If you have it, you will project it, and it will draw women as flowers draw bees.

Unfortunately, many men are actually afraid of women, and of sex. They consider their own natural impulses to be something dirty and sordid, and their guilts very often render them, if not impotent, then surely incompetent. Being a lover is not confined only to the bed; it requires constant care and nurturing in every other area of living.

That this happens is not beyond our comprehension. Even in this advanced day and age it somehow escapes many people that sex is not a dormant impulse that comes to life only after the marriage vows are spoken. Premarital sex is gazed upon as something unnatural when in effect the opposite is true. Society has attempted to drop a veil over single sex and all that it means. Society would have us believe that a boy and a girl can achieve puberty, with all its attendant body changes, without being affected. To expect this is to seek to impose crippling inhibitions on many among us.

Of late, happily, changes have come about. There is a tendency to recognize certain realities about single people, to accept certain behavior patterns not as evil but as normal and fruitful. Some men, carrying imposed burdens from their pre-puberty days, find it difficult to adjust, to lead a fulfilling sex life, to relate easily and rewardingly to young women. These men are often the "nicest" men, the ones many women might find most appealing and most desirable. I have heard many complaints from women of exactly this nature.

"I have a feeling," one pretty young thing told me recently, "that in a competitive social sutuation I never meet the men I would like the most. The pushy ones come crowding in squeezing the less agressive man away, never giving him or me a chance."

Obviously this is a fact of life. Men who are shy or socially insecure must find it within themselves to correct this situation. No one expects you to match the drive and competitive urge of your more aggressive brothers, but you can fight for your position in the sun. Don't quit so readily. Give the girl a chance to know you. Chances are you'll both be better off for it.

I have noticed that most men who are successful with women, successful, for that matter, in any social situation, have one trait in common. They look directly at the person to whom they are talking, or to whom they are *listening*. The latter, as any actor will tell you, is among the harder things to do. Pay attention to what other people say. Show your interest. They will respond positively to this. Concentrate on the woman you are with to the exclusion of all others. Let her know that you are interested. If you get weary of looking into her eyes then try some other portions of her face. Her nose, for instance, her eyes, her forehead, chin, ears, hairline. Hairlines are excellent to look at. They are generally irregular and therefore of some interest. Once you have noticed that *her* hairline is like no other, that her chin is different, that her ears are delicate pink shells, you will be able to tell her such tidbits in complimentary fashion. Italian men are given to paying considerable heed to a girl's mouth, informing her at intervals that it is a thing of great beauty, that it is a mouth like no other mouth, that it is a mouth they must feel under their own else die from frustration and anguish. I submit that this makes a man appear to be a very sexual animal indeed.

It is very easy to misunderstand a woman. She may appear quite the extrovert, yet in bed she will be shy and frightened. The contrary may also be true. Also, the fact that a woman appears extremely sensual and animalistic does not give a direct clue to how deep her sex drives run. Women too often are less interested in sex than they are in affection. A woman might give freely of her body to a man she likes, not caring whether or not she achieves an orgasm. To me, to most men, this indifferent attitude spoils the entire affair.

Women differ tremendously in their appetites. What will still hunger in one will serve only as an appetizer for another. Quantity has nothing to do with quality; often a compulsion for the former is only an indication of a lack of satisfaction. This, of course, applies to men as well. Many of us, male and female alike, use sex to prove themselves. It is one of our foremost devices for convincing ourselves that we are worthy. Unhappily it seldom works more than temporarily. If a man doesn't feel like a man a thousand conquests will not satisfy his ego.

To many such people sex is a weapon. It is a deadly one. We are all of us extremely vulnerable in this area. Women learn early to manipulate men in this fashion. And it is a wily man who finds he has the power to return the compliment. Withholding sex is using this weapon in its simplest form; women do it in many ways. A sudden desire to watch the Late Late Show is a sure sign. Constant headaches, or weariness are other common signals. As often as not, men have helped create the combinations of factors in women that produce these results. Most meen seem unaware of woman's needs and desires. It is a wise man indeed who learns enough about *one* woman to offer her emotional sustenance.

It's interesting to take note of the "ideal" woman. She apparently is actually a multitude of women, all different sizes, shapes and colors. As you may have noticed, girls with inflated bosoms do not dominate the world any more than their less amply endowed friends. Chestless women get married and have babies and enjoy sex with as much abandon, if not more, than the bosomy types. Men like girls of every conceivable shape and proportion. I suppose it's all based on your childhood; there is the man who likes fat, redheaded women because his mother was fat and redheaded, and there's the man who *loathes* fat, redheaded women because his mother was fat and redheaded. Go fight city hall.

You pays your money and you takes your choice.

Many men I've known make a rather basic mistake in their approach to women, as well as to life in general, in that they assume because a situation exists today it will also exist tomorrow. Moreover, that it will move inexorably toward preconceived goals. So that a kiss today means bed tomorrow; bed today means a "relationship"; a relationship inevitably means marriage. This is patently juvenile nonsense. It presupposes, on your part, that a woman finds you that fascinating that she is incapable of altering the curve of inevitability which you ascribe to life. Believe me, anxious as most women are to marry they are not desirous of making a mistake. A given woman may look upon you as a horrible mistake. This possibility may come to you as a terrible shock but it is worth accepting. You may be less than God's gift to the female sex.

A healthy realization of this reality will in fact make you much more attractive, and move you closer to your ideal image of yourself.

No less than the single girl, the single man should be charming. This simply means that he is concerned with other people, all people, and the ladies will clamor to do his bidding. He must be warm and affectionate, caring about others and the world around him. He will be tuned in to others' wave lengths, receptive to them, getting their messages no matter how communicated.

At all times, be a man. People should be aware of your maleness, your sexiness, your strength, your courage, your dependability, your tenderness, your compassion, simply because these are part of you. It is unnecessary to tell them. Don't toot your own horn. Let them judge the finished product for themselves. Like the writer who boasts of his greatness, the bragging lover still must prove himself where it counts.

As a man you will be an able interpreter. You will understand when "We'll see" means "yes," when "no" means "I need time" and when "No" means "yes." I had to learn the hard way. Many years ago after a long trying evening of thrust and parry with a delectable creature, I at last accepted her refusals as final. I prepared to leave.

"Stay," she said. "It's late and you can sleep here, if you promise to be good."

Overjoyed at not being forced to journey home in the wee hours when my office was but minutes from her apartment, I promised.

"You mean it?" she said. "Can I trust you?"

I crossed my heart and hoped to die before she was convinced. At last we went to bed, to the same bed. I kissed her good night, fought back the temptation for, after all, I had crossed my heart and hoped to die, rolled over and went to sleep. In the morning, I woke rested, proud but frustrated and went to work. Do you know, that girl never would speak to me again!

The moral of this story is that subways and beds are not always for sleeping.

CHAPTER SIX

IT'S YOUR AFFAIR ...

NICE GIRLS don't, is what people used to claim, but the sophisticated young man of today knows that the nicest girls do. This being so it is incumbent upon you to arrange a liason with a nice girl. Having done so you are expected to be nice to that nice girl.

It is my considered opinion that where you met her doesn't count, how long it took to locate a bed matters even less, and why she decided to succumb to your blandishments is probably the least important of all. Maybe she just had a sudden urge, or perhaps she thought this was the only way to get a charmer like you to see her again, or it might be that your glamor overwhelmed her (you are glamorous, aren't you, and rich and famous?), then again it was more likely your great and warm personality. It may have been any or all of these or something else entirely. Whatever it was it is behind you now.

There is only one question to ask yourself. Do you want to see her again? Not next year or even next week. But tomorrow, or the day after. If the answer is yes then by all means see her. Enjoy her. In bed and out. If you do, and we'll assume you do, you will probably be seeing her three or four times each week, to begin anyway. This will vary with your desire, strength and other obligations, social and otherwise.

Assuming you live alone, where you see her will be no problem. Unless she has some scruples against doing so (and many girls have), she will sleep at your place, leaving for work from there. This could possibly create a situation, to wit: it will be necessary for her to leave certain personal items in your apartment, possibly changes of clothing. You may feel this is an infringement on your privacy and cause you to feel some hostility toward your new friend. My advice is not to keep your distress to yourself. It will simply fester inside until it comes boiling over apropos of nothing into a battle royal which will end the affair in a most unsatisfying manner.

If you have really struck the mother lode you will have found yourself a girl who has been around. She will be far removed from virginity and will possess the skill and desire to please. If you have found one who lacks both the experience and the desire, my advice is to terminate the affair as quickly and painlessly as possible. I would suspect a wench who seems to know what she's doing yet takes no great pleasure in it. On the other hand, the lady with a naturally bawdy outlook can be taught any refinements that may appeal. Desire, as in football, is everything.

When attempting to instruct your bed partner in some of the more esoteric aspects of your mutual adventures, approach the subject by a circuitous route.

"Look, stupid, you ain't doing it right!" is not guaranteed to obtain the best results. A gentler tact is suggested. Proceed on the assumption that she is more than willing to learn, in fact wants you to teach her. Of course, this is all predicted on you knowing what it's all about. If you lack experience, then just let it go. Relax and have fun. Neither of you will know the difference.

The question of multiple affairs must be placed under close scrutiny. This must be handled strictly on an individual basis. Some men can and some men can't. A young man of but average physical and emotional stamina seeing a healthy young woman three times each week will have little need of or capacity for other females.

However, if the affair is somewhat more casual—perhaps you see your friend only once a week, or even less frequently—you may possess the wherewithal for other forays. This requires discipline and caution. One must never get dates confused, or call Miss X by Miss Y's name. That sort of thing is considered in horrible taste.

Women I have known have occasionally talked to me of their escapades and I'm aware that men boast of their conquests, past, present, and even hopes for the future, to a current paramour. Such bragging may prove to be disasterous. I must caution you never to put yourself in a position to force a woman to tell you the truth, the absolute truth, about yourself as a lover. Unless you were the first, she has undoubtedly known better. It figures. Time, if nothing else, enhances all things. It washes away the little frictions and annoyances that once seemed important. Yesterday's sweetheart is touched with nostalgia and you can't compete with that.

Some women have problems in bed that no man, repeat, no man, is going to solve. They are rooted too deeply in her psyche and her past. This is a job for the psychoanalyst's couch, not your bed. Do what you can for the poor dear. Suggest she seek help. Chances are powerful that she will look at you as if you recently crawled from under a rock.

"There's nothing wrong with *me*," will be her answer. Argument will be futile. Deposit her on her doorstep with a brotherly kiss on the brow. To sleep with a woman who gets nothing from the experience can put more of a strain on a man than he need bear.

If you have a continuing love affair with a girl, a good move would be to present her with a small present now and then. Something you can afford; no one expects you to go broke. But material manifestations of your affection will in no way hurt your standing. Flowers brought, for no particular reason, generally evoke a flood of warmth. There's something about flowers ... Naturally, if you can afford more expensive items, they are in order. No girl in her right mind will object to a neat string of pearls, or a diamond brooch, or a red Corvette. Things like that have a way of making a girl happy. However, should these be beyond your reach then a book she'd like to read, or a new Mort Sahl album, or a subscription to Realities, will do quite well.

If you have been spending most of your time at the lady's flat then an occasional bottle of hooch would be in order. You've probably been consuming most of hers.

If while wandering about town with her, you might see something in a store window that she's taken with, that you know would be perfect for her, like a cashmere cardigan. Go into that store. Buy her that sweater. You may eat nutted cheese sandwiches for lunch for a month, but you won't starve. She'll provide an abundance of nourishment to keep you going.

Bestowing gifts is a large part of the pleasure of a love affair. Once given, however, the sophisticated male never refers to them again. Especially not in anger. It wouldn't be at all smooth.

There are those uncouth lechers who once having bedded the object of their passion look upon her as little more than a chattel. Such a boor forgets she is human and female. He permits her to function as his personal maid. She cleans his apartment, sews on his buttons, does his laundry. She feeds his stomach regularly. In return for all this, he permits her to sleep with him. This isn't nice.

The female member of the affair is entitled to be treated with respect and consideration. She should be romanced to the best of your abilities. She enjoys eating in good restaurants, dancing, attending theatre or the movies. Take her to a concert or the ballet. It might not only do you good, you will enjoy it. And sharing these experiences will enhance your moments alone.

If, for whatever reason, you do not share the same bed on a given night, do not let her go home alone. Common practice, and it is *common,* current today, is to put a girl in a taxi with a couple of dollars and bid her good night. If she's worth being with she is worth seeing *safely* home. You want the privileges of a man; act like one.

Affairs, if they don't culminate in marriage, always run their course. They may simply terminate as a result of mutual lack of interest. A third party may come between you. Or a clash of personalities may send it up in flames, leaving only bitterness. Ending an affair with style may take as much skill and effort as starting one. The problem is to recognize the symptoms.

If your affair has gone wrong, if you and your beloved are continually having cat-and-dog fights (you know who the dog is, don't you?), if there is a cooling of her ardor, if she no longer *insists* on doing for you, then you'd better stand back and take a good look. Chances are you've had it. Perhaps it is only a temporary aberration on her part. It happens. She may have sworn to you in the beginning that the last thing in the world she wants is to be married. Marriage, she told you, is a destroyer of love (not necessarily), it is a killer of people, it ends freedom. Not for her this unhappy condition. But after a few months or so the condition seems less odious to her. The word seems emblazoned on the inside of her forehead. She peers past it at the world as if it were a monstrous neon sign overlooking Times Square. What's more, it keeps flickering on and off. A word from you would end her torment. But you don't want to get married. Under these conditions, I would terminate the relationship. It can get no better and both of you would be happier free to pursue your separate ambitions.

Resign yourself to this fact: all women want to get married. Even those who deny it, do. Even those who *keep* denying it, do. They just don't know better. From that vantage point you may assume that the average affair will run its course in from six months to a year. After half a year she begins to squirm. Her friends are plying her with questions as to your intentions. If they don't include marriage, they will ask her slyly, why is she letting you waste her time? Notice the insidious phrasing utilized. No accident there. All the onus is heaped upon you. She is not wasting her time, you are doing it for her. Oh, but they are clever!

Now begin the manipulations. You will phone her and there will be no answer and—at midnight. She will suggest that you date other women—and she other men. She will withhold sex intermittently, though she will be positively overwhelmed with your prowess when you do make love.

"Oh, darling," is the general approach, "how sad it is."

"What is?" you will offer at the bait.

"That it all must end."

"What must end?"

"All this. And it's so special, what we have together."

You'll go home thinking about that. It will worry you. What the hell has she got in mind? To put you on the defensive, that's what.

If you haven't proposed to her within a reasonable period of time after the above campaign has been launched, then you must be prepared to fend off the final attack. She will propose to you in unmistakable terms. At this point it should be noted that most marriages take place because women propose to men. If they waited for us to make the move nothing might ever happen. This does not mean that you must succumb. However, once the ultimate gesture has been made it's all over but the playing of Lohengrin, or your exit music.

Actually, she is right. An extended affair does get to a point of diminishing returns. There is only one step left, marriage and the beginning of an entirely different way of life for you. So don't vacillate. In or out. Marry the girl or break it off. Anything else is unhealthy.

It may very well be that your reluctance to marry is not a basic issue with you at all. To the contrary, perhaps unconsciously you really do want to marry. But this girl is not the girl you want to marry. Instinctively you retreat from forming a permanent alliance with her. Her neuroses don't jibe with your own, and vice versa. Not everybody can make it with everybody else. It may give you a wrench or two to break it off but it will reward you both. Give yourself a chance to find someone else to care about. You will. And the odds are you'll be just as miserable with her.

Now it's over. You have irrevocably, once-and-for-all broken off. What do you do? You sit home and worry yourself to death, most likely. Big mistake. Phone all your friends immediately. Let them know that you are back in circulation. Demand that they get their girl friends to arrange dates for you. Make the rounds again. Find another likely prospect. Don't brood. Such negativism is terribly destructive.

You will not be able to leave your gloom at home. Instead you will wear it like a cape everywhere you go, including your job. You will make mistakes, set back your career by months if not years. Glum young men are not looked on with favor by most companies. Happy is as happy does! Keep smiling! Every man a tiger!

So hit the beaches hard, men. Don't be thrown by a single setback. Circulate. Help the pain dissipate itself. However, should nothing help, I would suggest attempting to return to your last friend. Perhaps you can reclaim the affair, if it bugs you that much. This is not a book on how to get married, or even why, to get married, but the author recognizes its tremendous fascination for anyone unmarried. After all, one is always attracted to the untested areas of life. One must also confess that numberless first-class lechers have succumbed with no visible injury. Rubirosa, whose activities with a variety of ladies, were headlined in tabloids all over the world, married and has never been heard of since, except in relation to revolutions and such.

I truly believe that lechery may be focused on one woman with huge gobs of success, if the right female is involved. This, however, as those offerings to sell which come from brokerage houses point out, is not an offering to sell. To obtain the prospectus ...

CHAPTER SEVEN

THE GOOD LIFE

IT IS LIVED at many levels and in a variety of ways. No two men go about it in the same manner. You may get your jollies by traipsing around in a white Jaguar with an antiseptic blond in the adjoining bucket seat. Your buddy finds it more fulfilling to chauffeur a lusty, busty black-haired piece of fluff about in a native-built jalopy that allows him room for action. You bets your money and you takes your choice.

Whichever way you play, it's an open game. Anyone can sit in. The rules are very simple, to wit: the more you bet the more you can win. To put it another way, live your life to the fullest. Each day is part of your life, taste it, take a big, big bite out of it and let the juice trickle down your chin. Experience and sensation are part of that life. So is satisfaction. Live today for today, but with an eye on tomorrow, for it will come.

The fear that cripples most of us is not the fear of death but the end of life. People too often play it safe to the point of absurdity. They hold their cards so close to the vest that no one can read them, including themselves. I find that even in mistakes and unpleasantness there is profit. And I am no Pollyanna. Rather, I feel that while being pinched may bring a degree of pain it is a reminder that I have feelings and am alive.

"What are you doing?" is a question often asked.

"Killing time," is an answer too often received. What a deadly confession that is. Killing time. As if time is inexhaustible, will go on forever for the individual. It runs out for us all and to kill it is to destroy a part of yourself. People find it much easier to escape from life than to meet it head on. Don't run away. Don't become detached. It is surrendering to death. Get involved in life. Do things. Go places. Work to fulfill an ambition you may have.

At a party some years ago, I met a man of forty-two who revealed in the course of the evening's conversation that he had just enrolled in night school, seeking his bachelor's degree. He had decided that he wanted to teach. Another man, a much younger man, asked scornfully: "How can you waste all that time? It will take at least six years."

I've always remembered the answer, which was offered with a benign smile: "Well, if I don't go to school I surely won't have the degree in six years."

Today that man is teaching in a high school and his contentment and sense of fulfillment beggars description. Years, I submit, have nothing to do with age. Senility often infects the young. The aged frequently have time enough to do anything; the young seldom find time for anything.

A mistake many young men make is to set up comparisons between themselves and others of comparable years. John at twenty-six is already a vice-president of a public relations company while I am merely a copywriter at Cunningham & Walsh, is the familiar plaint. Or the would-be playwright who measures himself against those who are already successful on Broadway. To make such comparisons is self-defeating. Each man is unique. Each of us sets his own pace, marching to the sound of his own drummer.

It is the unique quality in each of us that matters. Exploit that as fully as you can. Reach for your particular horizon; having achieved it you will find another horizon draws you on. As you develop as a man your horizons will stretch wider before you. But your success or failure is in no way connected with that of another man, whether known to you or not.

So it is with women. See to your own desires. It isn't a contest to be won by he who runs up the highest score. And satisfaction isn't derived from how many orgasms you have. One may bring you more pure joy than half-a-dozen bring another man.

Do things. Get out in the world, by yourself, if necessary. The interested man is the interesting man. The more you experience the more satisfaction you will gain. Don't succumb to external pressures. Live your life according to the dictates of your own needs. Let your uncles, aunts, parents, sisters, brothers, nieces, nephews and so on lead their lives and you lead yours. What they want generally has nothing to do with you, though they might like it otherwise.

As was mentioned earlier in these pages, this is not an invitation to you to lay aside any of your convictions and live in any particular manner. It is instead, I hope, a clear-eyed view of the world in which we live, especially in regard to the romping about of single men and women. What you do about it is your own affair.

It can be a good life, if one can accept it for what it is, not what he would like it to be. It is important, in maintaining a mental attitude geared to the conquest of women, that a man take care of himself, physically and mentally. That means some exercise, physical and mental. Flabbiness of mind and body is not conducive to playing the game of lechery successfully.

The single man overflowing with life will find that sex plays a healthy, active part in it. Women will respond to him because, being vibrantly alive, he makes them feel more alive. It's a self-perpetuating cycle.

By using life, rather than letting it use you, you will enjoy it more. Be alert to the constantly shifting scenes of life around you. Just a moment ago, for example, a lovely young creature ambled past my window, walking her dog. I suspect the dog is a miniature Schnauzer. I must confirm that suspicion. She's some distance down the block now so I must hurry after her. I wouldn't want to miss this opportunity to enlarge my fund of knowledge.

See what I mean?

PART TWO

CHAPTER EIGHT

"Freud taught us the significance of sex in relation to human happiness; Kinsey has taught us that sex convention is one thing and practice another."

—DR. ABRAM KARDINER

SEX WITHOUT MARRIAGE is no more a question than it is an answer; instead it is a subject, and a vital one in almost all senses of the dictionary meaning. This, of course, has eternally been true, but for many pre-Freud pre-Kinsey years the problems inevitably connected with non-marital sex were looked upon as indecent—best to be ignored or taken up with the family doctor or clergyman, if Mother and Father couldn't handle them. In any event, Mother, Father, the medical profession and the clergy were all, however human and humane, ill-prepared for dealing with the subject realistically. Mores and custom made it clear that sex without marriage was a sadly improper state of affairs, if not downright unnatural. All this began to change with the emancipation of women and the discovery of sex as a pleasure principle as well as the only functional means of populating the world. Which means, since women have not been out of their shackles too long, custom and mores—and women themselves—still bear the marks of bondage, and, until very recently, the recognition of the existence of sex as such, with or without marriage, has belonged to the psychiatrists, sociologists, and anthropologists, and the minority group of the far-sighted and far-thinking who were students of these sciences themselves, wittingly or not.

The concept of sex as belonging exclusively to the married state is, from the long historical view, also recent. In the sixteenth century, for instance, the kind of sexual fastidiousness—shy daintiness that made a mockery of the word modesty—was unheard of. Chastity had its values, as it has always had and probably always will have, so long as the world's society is based upon Western civilization's idea of family and tribe. But chastity itself was not, in the sixteenth century, anything more than a desirable state; those who fell by the wayside were not ostracized, or even criticized. They were indulged in the same way that present-day society indulges the person who doesn't "quite make it" as a business success. All this changed during Queen Victoria's long reign—when sex itself was all but virtually eliminated. Had not the Church pointed out that procreation was a moral duty, the human race might well have ended then and there! Such was the threat to Nature of the Victorian Era, having borrowed along the way from other rule-making societal groupings, such as the Puritans, who for reasons of religious persuasion or affairs of state chose to ignore Nature and institute dictums of their own whim.

Nearly fatal to mankind—and womankind—these false precepts, like many others, left ruin and dessication in their wake. But reality and the basic life-drives do not succumb so easily; there is always the individual who looks flatly at the flat truth, and in time reality survives. So it has done in the twentieth century, and though the critics of morals and morality are stringent, strident and sturdy, the fact remains that there are more and more thoughtful people aware that the sex drive is as basic as hunger and that it will not be put down by haloed-religiosity, custom, or wishful thinking. Each mortal, male or female, has a sexual necessity; such alack, alas, or welcome, Life has decreed.

This, being the case, now that we have had Freud in our midst, Kinsey in our faces, and countless others gnawing at our wits, what do we do? We accept Sex—withal. And what does this mean?

Sex, or the sexual drive, being basic, as almost no one can now effectually deny, must be coped with. And it is all very good and well to advocate marriage as the aegis under which to gratify this drive, but real life strongly points out that marriage alone cannot take care of the whole thing—i.e., there are those who have never been married and may never marry (yet the sexual drive exists); there are those who have been married and are no longer married who will never marry again (divorced or widowed); there are those for whom the marriage potential still exists, but—until that time—must deal with the problem of their sexuality, their natural human drives.

In this country, at the last census, there were over 63-and-a-half million women of a sexually mature age. The male figure was somewhat less. The "somewhat less" indicates that there are more hands up for proposal than there are hands to take them. This includes all categories of women: the over fourteens, widows, college girls, happily marrieds, unhappily marrieds, spinsters, women separated, women divorced, and those whose husbands are absent from home for one reason or another. However, of the 63-and-a-half million women, around 26 million are at large! This does not mean to imply that our fair land is ravaged by 26 million slightly tamed wild beasts, all yearning for Sadie Hawkins Day, but it does mean that a body of women sufficient to exclusively occupy three cities the population size of New York have sexual needs and no marital means for answering them.

Ideally, of course, it would benefit society and help to stabilize the national economy if these 26 million women could be paired off with the available opposite male number, raiding other countries to make up the deficit. Then there would be no sex without marriage—though unquestionably there would be an increase of marriage without sex. But Mother Nature is a far more headstrong, whimsical old gal than Mother Public, and has to date always had her way. Consequently, Mother Public must do the compromising.

The growth of the world's population has made it more necessary than ever to successfully provide means for keeping the sexually mature but unmarried segment of the population at peace and controlled, but the efforts to date have been small, timorous, and largely ineffectual ... largely guided by Need, which operates as blindly as a hungry animal seeking food, rather than by Wisdom or informed common sense. The steps that have been taken have been made at the social level—the YWCA and similar organizations which undertake to shelter, feed and match-make for the unmarried, marriageable female—and, to some scant extent, at the legal level—many states which had outrageously outdated laws governing marriage, divorce and even sexual habits have removed these from their statutes. (For an example of a preposterous law which still existed in the twenties, it was illegal for a *man and wife* to practice sexual intercourse on Sundays in Arkansas! God pity, then, the man and non-wife who did so, though this must have been a difficult law to enforce in any case.) But State Legislatures and YWCAs cannot solve the whole problem alone. What is needed, on every level—Family, Church, and State—is a realistic understanding of the basic human drives and the price that Nature will inevitably exact if these basic drives are starved or ignored. No legislation in the world, even with the combined forces of

Family, Church, and State, can successfully stamp out or bring to heel the human need for sexual expression.

How, then, can a controlled outlet be established—since an acceptable one has not—been simply "found"—for the needs, say, of some 26 million females who have at this moment no husbands? As with all basic instincts, the gratification must always, in the final analysis, be left to the individual with her individual requirements. All society can do is lend an intelligent assist where needed. In the matter of sex without marriage, more attention, and from a different slant, must be paid to sex education, starting at home and going upward through church, school and the adult world where love, marriage, birth and death are on the everyday common exchange. While it was the order of the day for the Victorian mother to tell her daughter that she would one day be married and become a mother herself, even so that Victorian mother must have been wistfully crossing her fingers hoping that her promise would come true. Consequently, if such a fate was largely a fiction in those strict moral times, what of such a mother's promise today? No woman in her right mind should prophesy with certainty the marriage-and-children outcome for her daughter's life. It is even questionable if such a destiny is now or will continue to be the ideal destiny. Flatly stating that it is will not make it so, any more than it will make such a destiny come true. Twenty-six million women can, at present, at least, bear witness to this.

Far better, then, that we rephrase our teachings to the female young on the subject of love and marriage. It should be made clear to the girl child, as soon as she is capable of clarifying information in her own mind, that while every baby is the creation of a mommy and a daddy, mommy and daddy are not of Nature's necessity Mr. and Mrs. The child should learn that procreation and sexual communion between male and female are the only contributions which Nature makes—any others are man-made. In this way perhaps the Dark Ages of Sexual Enlightenment can be dispersed, and future generations of women can come to accept the sexual need and function as casually and as serenely as the other basic drives. Then sex without marriage will truly be left up to the individual to cope with naturally and intelligently, just as sex in marriage is, for the most part, a private affair.

CHAPTER NINE

SEX. One of the biggest little words in the language, and part of any post-infant vocabulary. But what is sex? It is, primarily, one of the two divisions of organisms: in its second dictionary meaning, it pertains to the distinctive function of the male or female in reproduction. And in its third popular meaning, sex is conjugal union which may or may not result in reproduction. At no place in any dictionary will sex be defined as legal marriage.

But sex has other meanings and connotations too—also not found in the dictionary. Sex very often means sexual attraction, or that which is desirable to the physical senses. Things, places, and people—including animals other than humans—have all been described as looking sexy, sounding sexy, etc. Purists and pure grammarians may feel affronted at this liberty-taking, but the obvious need for such a word—a need that sensuous and sensual alone or combined do not fill—has created the widespread use of "sexy" to describe the sensuous, sometimes, the sensual, sometimes, and that third quality for which no previous word existed, a quality which often embodies the older, more acceptable words, enhances them, or supersedes them altogether. Therefore, in any book about sex without marriage, it is important that every aspect of sex in all of its definitions and nuances of meaning be considered. As anyone knows, for instance, saying that someone is sexy does not mean that that person is 1) sexual (we are all sexual) 2) that he or she is oversexed—or so sexually potent that all other qualities of character, personality and appearance are dwarfed to the point of invisibility 3) or that the person has a voracious hunger for sex with no appetites apart from those to do with conjugal union. In current parlance, sexiness equates more closely to vivid good health and normality than it does with anything else. Any vivacious girl over fourteen (and often under) can be and usually is classified as sexy. Sexiness then is closely allied to high spirits; bodily fitness and charm. And not even the tightest and most strait-laced Victorian lady would do more than blush prettily if she were accused of possessing these qualities.

SEX AND NATURE

Sex is necessary, but is it natural? The Victorian lady would probably say no, but these days she would be put down on all sides. However, there is much disagreement—and with just cause— about what constitutes "natural" sex. Some authorities go so far as to say that if it is sex it is natural, regardless of how it expresses itself, and that any boudoir gymnastics with any partner are okay; a sort of sex unlimited point of view. Here Convention goes in for some vigorous headshaking, and rattles out that old quotation about Nature abhorring a vacuum, thus indicating that she, (and it) does not approve of extremes.

Sexual rites that are sexual wrongs are usually extremes: bestiality, necrophilia, infantaphilia, etc. If one considers such sexual practises unnatural—or abnormal, at best—grounds for so doing would seem to lie in the fact that in all cases when human beings take to wife (or husband) animals, dead animals and humans, dead young animals or live young animals or humans, there is little or no prospect for sexual response, not to say understanding, on the part of partners in these categories, and certainly no prospect for anything along the reproductive line to come of it. Perhaps those who indulge in such sexual diversions could and do argue that the non-reproductive aspect is one in its favor; or, as in the limerick about the necrophiliac from Belgrave who put to sexual use the corpse of a prostitute, look at the money saving. Non-involving, neat and clean as some of these sex habits may be, even were they legal, there are drawbacks that discourage, disgust, and frighten all but the most intrepid of explorers into the far regions of sex, and most people would agree that Aleister Crawley was one Aleister Crawley too many.

However, ruling out non-human or sub-human sex practices, there are still many possibilities for sexual coupling that are generally considered abnormal—i.e., incest and homosexuality, to name two. Are these unnatural? Scientific opinion would seem to indicate that they are natural enough, but abnormal in our society, abnormal meaning above normal, or removed from it. But abnormal doesn't mean subnormal. Clearly, though natural, homosexuality and incest are abnormal, and they are so only because they are not the norm in Western culture.

Norms in any culture are created by supply and demand. Ours being fairly well balanced numerically between the two sexes, anything that threatens to run away with the pattern is a threat, good or bad, to the pattern. A large outbreak of homosexuality in the culture could seriously effect the economy, to say nothing of the birthrate, and it is, therefore, to the body of society, what a wildly spreading group of cancer cells are to the human and animal organism: if it doesn't kill it off entirely, it considerably changes it. This should be, though it isn't, the chief objection to homosexuality. And in this time of concern about the population explosion, an outbreak of homosexuality in those areas most troubled with too much output of human kind might prove an asset (it has been seriously suggested—in *Harper's* magazine—as a solution to the problem). But homosexuality remains not only an abnormality to society, but one as illegal as incest.

Even the methods of homosexual intercourse—sodomy, which includes fellatio, pederastry—are against the law, whether practiced by husband and wife or anybody else!

Considering that homosexuality as a recognized and legal sexual expression has existed and continues to do so in many other countries and cultures throughout the world, it would seem that its severe punishment by our law and society is not only out of keeping with our talent for freedom and fondness for liberality, but anachronistic. Why are we so afraid of it? Its legalization would not necessarily threaten marriage and the family or appreciably alter the birthrate (heterosexuality is here to stay), and if it is "wrong," why is it?

Again it would seem that if there is any valid objection possible, it must be on the grounds that the sexual act in homosexuality cannot, biologically, result in reproduction. This objection can similarly be applied to incest, along with others, the slight difference being that though reproduction is possible biologically, it is not desirable socially. It was once strictly thought that incest was also biologically dangerous, as well as socially undesirable, but this conclusion has been reopened for investigation. In any event, society wants no part of it either, has laws against it, and is taking no chances. The practice of incest—especially between siblings—is a rarity among adults, though a great deal goes on between children, and parents and children. It poses such a slight problem for the general public, that arguments for and against, if presented here, would be unnecessary temporizing.

With the exception of lesbianism and onanism, any non-scientific survey of sex without marriage, as it applies to women, can dispense with full coverage of sexual variations of an unusual nature. And in the case of masturbation as a sex-without-marriage outlet, since its practice seldom interferes with marriage or precludes it, the study of it, or even the rate of its incidence, is relatively unimportant in a general viewing of the non-marital sex scene.

Lesbianism, however, does interfere with and preclude marriage in many cases, but an examination of lesbianism as opposed to heterosexuality is a separate subject. Sex without marriage, as discussed here, is chiefly concerned with how heterosexual sex drives are met with outside matrimonial bonds, and not with the merits and drawbacks of other sex drives, natural, abnormal or not. Homosexuality and other sexual abberations are, for this survey, regarded as sexual substitutes.

Girl dogs, cats, elephants, hamsters, and whales, can and do get around for weeks on end throughout the year without the slightest urge for copulation. This is because their sexual urge moves in strict cycles, and the purpose of these cycles is apparently for reproductive goals entirely. It may be observed that far more false pregnancies, for instance, occur in the lower mammals than among humans. In any event, the human female from time of menstruation through menopause (and sometimes both before and after) is normally fertile during one period within every month. It is possible that her sexual urges are more intense during the time of her fertility, but it is also true that her sexual urges never entirely disappear at any given time. In other words, most females are receptive to sexual union 365 days a year, however such receptivity may vary. But, unlike other basic appetites— such as hunger, survival instinct, etc.—the sexual force, however strong, is so subtle that it seems undemanding, and is perhaps the easiest of all the basic drives to sublimate. Hunger strikes are almost solely the province of religious or labor fanatics, but sexual continence is practised far and wide, and, except when undertaken for religious reasons, pretty much a private matter. However, there is no sexually fulfilled man or woman—married or single—who does not pity the virgin spinster, somehow, or the

Catholic priest. Why? Because total sexual abstinence is unnatural and because it is a hardship, since sex is the life force and as necessary to total well-being as a balanced diet.

But how is a sexual balanced diet to be achieved? Of the 26 million women living singly, about 12 million are indeed single— i.e., have not entered into a legal married state. This group, of course, includes nuns and virgin spinsters and others who have elected, for one reason or another, to go to their graves untouched by human male hand; but the majority of the number are young women of marriageable age, and it is with this group that there is the most concern. Most of these women will marry or will certainly want to, since marriage is still society's solution for the pursuit of life and happiness, but what about sexual activity for this group before marriage, or if ultimately there is none?

This question, alas, is not so private or individual as it should be, or would seem. Society and its arbiters have wildly conflicting opinions about sexual behavior for the unmarried female of marriageable age—a good thing, undoubtedly, for in our very recent past, society dictated but one course of action for this person: nonaction. Today, however, depending upon the community, the family within the community, and the individual within the family, prescribed sexual activity can range all the way from experimentation amounting to promiscuity to Nothing At All.

Good advice to the unmarried person who finds herself in doubt as to what is sexually right and what is downright sexually wrong is to use good common sense. The price for going against society's grain has always come high, and is as unavoidable as death and taxes. However, society has ceased to be of such a piece as it once was, and what may be unforgiveable in one community may be tolerated or taken as natural in another. The girl who would go sexually exploring would do well to consider her terrain: if she comes from a very religious family, is still in it, or involved in it, she would do well to curb her sexual appetites until marriage, whatever her own personal beliefs about morals and sex may be. Failing this, she should strike out on her own and find a new home where people are more compatible. If this is not possible, and if she is bravely determined to lead her own life, discretion is her only hope. Any of these courses—continence, breaking away, or caution—is difficult, but the question of sexual decorum is one which nearly every female must face.

If the unmarried girl is a member of a community or family where cultural liberality and permissiveness rule, her decision for or against pre-marital or non-marital sex can be as difficult—and more complex—than her religiously-bound counterpart's. Discovering just *how* permissive is permissive may call for a great deal of perception and ingenuity, and may result in some painful blundering and punishment. Lip service and action are galaxies apart, and it may very well be that the mother who prides herself upon her informality, her openness with her children, their enlightened education, will turn into a screaming vilifier if her daughter dares to practise what Mother preached. The daughters of these women would do well to cut Mamma in on their sexual plans or hopes from the beginning; often the reason for the liberal mother's regression is that her feelings are hurt by no longer being confided in and treated like a pal. In any event, most mothers are minutely and seriously concerned with their daughter's future and happiness, and while Mother may not know best, she, as a mother and a wife has the advantage of at least knowing something about sex first hand, and if the daughter is sensible, listening to what her mother has to say on the subject may be useful on many levels. For instance, if the mother is not an utter fool she can gauge far better usually than her daughter the possible reaction her daughter's behavior would have on the rest of the family, on the community, and on her daughter's future.

As for those young women who are the products of parents who say, "Don't do as I do, do as I say," they are most often forced into open defiance or stealth if they go their own sexual way. Therefore, while it is comparatively easy for the child of strictly religious parents to know what her parents and her world really think and feel about sexual freedom, it is a much more hit or miss estimate that the progressive product has to make without actual experimentation—and, too, parental opinions vary widely with the sexual situation—which would make it seem, indeed, that it takes many more than two to tango: it takes a whole world to make such a pairing possible.

<h2 style="text-align:center">THE OPPOSITE NUMBER</h2>

He, the opposite number, doesn't have to be Mr. Right or Mr. Wrong, but usually time alone properly evaluates which, if either, he is.

Since most sexual experience for the young woman of marriageable age takes place while the girl is under the family roof, not only its extent but the choice of her partners is usually a reflection of family and community ideas and influence. Her convictions are secondary, and what she thinks of as her tastes and preferences may very well alter considerably after she is on her own. This is equally true for her opposite number, the young man of marriageable age, still living at home, or just starting out.

Both are the products of a peculiar time in the history of morality, and the confusions of issues reopened or opened and shaken of their mustiness for the first time, or decisions reversed present all the chaos and hysteria of a formerly smooth-running, well-directed railroad terminal where schedules, tracks and trains were reshifted overnight. So the opposite number is as much in it as she is—and he is no longer so certain either that it is a man's world. As things go in the future, it may or may not be. For this reason alone, today's Gay Seducer is hardly so devil-may-care as he was reputed to be fifty years ago. The illegitimate birth rate of today counts far fewer babies whose mothers were victims of men "having their way" with them. Quite often it was the other way around. One young woman, unmarried, who found herself pregnant, was astonished when a friend suggested that the father-to-be should have a say-so in the matter. "I don't want to marry him!" she exclaimed. "So why should he be consulted?"

Most unmarried mothers-to-be, or unmarried women who run the risk of becoming such, do not have such bizarre, inde-pendent—and wholly selfish—opinions concerning their sexual partners. But it is true that sexual intercourse is now, outside marriage, closer to becoming a fifty-fifty proposition.

While young men are undoubtedly more sexually free than are young women, their attitude is far less flippant and shallow toward the girl who says yes than in days gone by. Society also punishes the male of the species if things go amiss. The young man of good family who is in love with the young girl of good family does almost as much thinking of the pros and conse-quences of sexual alliance without marriage as she does. And so do his parents, both sides of the family are in on it—or in for it—these days. If possible, sex is a more serious business than ever.

THE SEXUAL GOURMAND AND THE SEXUAL GOURMET

Making a choice as to which to be, or on which side to line up and how close to the end or middle, is usually not one which confronts the unmarried girl at home. Instead, it is the concern of the more sexually mature woman—one of that group of some 14 million who must ask herself that paradoxical question, "Am I single if I've been married?" and then decide what her answer means and what it will lead to. If she answers that she is single but not separate, beyond doubt she has no intention of taking the sexual veil. The question here of present-day morality—sexual right-doing and sexual wrong—is as complex and almost as difficult as it is for her younger counterpart. Instead of parental protection and guidance, the ex-wife has only experience and conscience to guide her—both of which can be woefully and willfully wrong, and she will have only herself to blame!

The widows, the divorcees, deserted wives, deserted mistresses, the legally separated, and those whose husbands are so consistently absent for business or other reasons that a sex life is nonexistent, usually find they have a conscious need for sexual companionship and, moreover, a desire for marriage or a marriage-like relationship with one man. Going about creating a new sexual outlet for her needs presents a crater full of dilemmas. She, too, has society and status symbols to consider, and she may have family—her own—as well. Further, she knows that few eligible men consider sexual dalliances with has-beens and left-overs—however attractive such may be—on the same par of serious consequence, or any consequence, as an affair with a less-tired, and often less true, younger partner. Sex, for those who have been there, very often has all the aspects of a game, and not much more meaning. For something meaningful to develop, much more effort and thought and planning must go into a relationship. And the cheery, brave little axiom, "If at first you don't succeed, try, try again!" is more likely to cause mouth corners to turn down rather than up when this prospect is in the view of the ex-married would-be-married-again contestant. It is exasperating, demeaning and frustrating for the woman who tries to get back into the swim and finds herself again and again thrown out of it. What is wrong with her? Nothing is usually the answer, except that she may expect too much. This would-be

SEX WITHOUT MARRIAGE

sexual gourmet may eventually find herself, bottle in hand, saying to hell with it, and sadly going down the glutton's drain. Or, if her will power is superior to her tenacity and optimism, she may become so frugal with her sexual indulgences that gourmet or gourmand is no longer the issue—she will have dieted herself, through false pride, into sexual starvation.

These conditions of too much or too little may tease the minds and emotions of the ex-married sexual abstainers, but they do not constitute problems. Is it better then to marry or to burn? Every woman must make this decision according to her own morals and her own needs. The gods take pity on her within whom desire and moral belief conflict! The chances are that she will spend the rest of her life favoring first one and then the other, without reconciliation, reaping remorse on both sides of the scale.

All this is not to say that many ex-married women find they must have affairs in order to restore themselves to the married state—if that is their goal. But certainly women in urban communities know that the pressures for non-marital sex are strong. What does it matter anyway? is the casual attitude. The answer again is long and complicated and strictly personal. Some women should definitely go to work honing down their scruples; others should strive to build them up fortress size, and no sand castles permitted! The tortures of doubt which assail the non-married non-virgin would, if amplified, drown out a good part of the other cries of woe in the world.

THE LONE WOLVERINE (GENDER FEMALE)

Usually this is a gal who has looked marriage, or its equivalent, in the face and when the image has faded has given a philosophical shrug. She may be classified as a sexual gourmand or a sexual gourmet—depending, more often than not, on who is doing the classifying—but one thing is sure: she is still sexually viable and has come to terms of one kind or another with herself. Usually, too, she will belong to the 30 to 40 (plus) age group, will be earning her own living, or lifting her own scissors to clip her own coupons, living alone, or in peaceful compromise with others; and, above all, she will be, in varying degrees, glad she is alive.

How does she get this way? She gets this way through sense and sensibility, trial and error, and an abiding faith in herself and her own usefulness. At some important point in her life she takes that grab bag full of decisions deferred and calmly considers them all, ripping up here, piecing back together there, pondering this one, laughing at that one—settling, in other words, the major issues of life as applied to her personally. Sex without marriage, of course, is one of them. Is it to be or not to be? The Lone Wolverine is not just a girl who can't say no, but one who realizes that for the sake of her own psyche, persuasions, habits and hopes, her best answer is yes.

How does this sexually emancipated creature manage sex without marriage? In much the same spirit and in much the same way as her male counterpart. She takes it as it comes along, judging each sexual involvement on its own merits. She detaches, perforce, sex from all its moral and legal-marital moorings and regards it as a pleasure device entirely; she does this knowing the risks involved—knowing she can drown in a whirlpool of passion, should she misjudge her own strength and character, or those of her partners; knowing that "sticky situations" will arise time and time again from which she must extricate herself; knowing the force of society's will and wrath against indiscreet transgressors who must drift on its mercy.

Why does she decide for this instead of looking for marriage, or waiting docilely on the sidelines? Because her make-up and nature and experience are such that she knows she is a better functioning human being as an Independent Woman. This does not preclude warmth, love of home, husband and children, but it does mean she has taken stock and found herself essentially sufficient unto herself. She must, in other words, wear the pants in the family, and since society still vetoes this as a womanly role and causes suffering to man, woman and child in a home dominated by the wife, the sensible strong woman lives her own life in her own way—unless she has the unlikely luck of meeting her match or male superior. Consequently, the mature non-married non-virgin who tells you she does not want to get married, is quite contented with life as she is living it, can get along on her own, is very likely telling the truth. If and when she ever remarries, or marries, you may be sure her reasons for doing so are lengthy and sane and go far beyond "Because I love him," though undoubtedly this one will be included too.

THE BITCH IN HEAT, or the Non-Profit Prostitute

This creature, when engaged upon a course of sex without marriage, very often can be found barking up the wrong tree. She would be far happier in a kennel where she is sure to get what she is after, for her quest is not just for a stud, or for a home, but for offspring. And, sadly enough, often she doesn't herself know it. But to the experienced, male and female alike, she can be spotted a mile off. Her disposition is almost always "bitchy"—i.e., she snarls at other females, is on no account to be trusted; and, with the male, she pulls out all the stops and lets go full blast to entice him, with about as much care for him, once she is safely gotten with young, as a black widow spider.

In her blind desperation she will go anywhere, to any lengths, and is willing to turn the same stone a dozen times to satisfy her craving. Unfortunately, this earth girl is as crafty as she is dedicated, though she often succeeds in outwitting herself, too. Her disguises are as numerous as a movie star's wardrobe, and she can be a perfect chameleon—undetectable and undefinable to the naive and unshaded eye. She, the sexually unharnessed bitch in heat, is little better than a predator. When the fits are on her, "there's just nothing she won't do." She may make grand sport for the heartless hunter, but she may well become a pitiful burden to society—an unwed mother or a non-profit prostitute.

Strangely enough, the bitch in heat—the woman whose sexual drive is determined to go all the way—is as much of an abnormality as she is a menace when she operates outside the sexual moral law. (Usually, her compulsions being what they are, she easily and early lands a mate—and almost any mate will do—who keeps her barefooted and pregnant.) And she is a ruthless abnormality when her mating call has not been answered or her appetites have not been satisfied, and as puzzled about it all as a visitor to the fourth dimension. Usually frigid, however fertile, her appeasement lies in gravidity, her climax in childbirth travail, and her hope, after the delivery room, back on the couch again. This woman, when married, contributes as many human lives as possible to this over-populated world, if little else. (She usually makes a lousy mother.) Seemingly, she is Nature's darling, but in addition to being frigid, she is sometimes sterile; if she is spouseless as well, she presents, perhaps, the saddest spectacle of all those who engage in sex without marriage.

The haunts and watering places of this pathetic however interesting species are easy to find: wherever the boys are. As she ages and loses her attractiveness, she usually frequents bars, and adds dipsomania to her nymphomania. In her grief and frustration, she feeds hyena-like on any male available and may often be found in the company of such misfits as pimps, drunkards,

Don Juans, Sporting Husbands and Ancient Mama's Boys. Depending on her intellect age and physical charms, she sometimes upgrades the line by adding homosexuals and perennial ex-husbands to her diet.

Needless to say, such a person should be taken firmly by the hand at the beginning, led back into captivity, measured for a chastity belt and a skullcap made to a headshrinker's measurements. But the potter's hand having shook, shakes on; she is wily and hard to catch, and hides—usually successfully if the bottle has not gotten to her—out in the open, masquerading as a healthy, normal woman. Though far more deeply neurotic than her Wolverine sister, if she thinks of her plight at all, or considers it one, she blames everyone but herself and is a cruel critic of other ladies of easy virtue.

The Bitch in Heat, the would-be mother eternally in quest of fertilization, makes a travesty of motherhood and the maternal instinct. She is much too much of a good thing and far more prevalent in her number than would seem possible.

KINSEY, FREUD AND THE FUTURE

Statistics indicate that a good percentage of women who have once been married will marry again (the 14 million group) and a girl's chances for getting married at all—though the male population of aged 14 and up lags in number by some half million behind the female—are better than fifty-fifty. Population distribution between male and female has much to do with sexual morality and custom and its maintenance. It is Dr. Abram Kardiner's observation that moral codes and ethics change eventually when they no longer benefit society. We will probably, therefore, have our present-day marriage conventions for a long time to come, though sexual taboos have been greatly ameliorated and will continue to be altered to fit the times and the radically changing culture. It is most unlikely that Americans will ever adopt polygamy—this occurs in countries where men are really at a premium—or that we will, as a nation, ever be obliged to follow the example of the polyandrous Marquesans, where every wife has at least two husbands. The chances are, barring cataclysmic disorder, that the population growth will continue to divide itself in more or less the same proportions between male and female.

As for sex without marriage, the Kinsey report may have revealed some startling information along these lines as well as others, but the fact that non-marital sexual practice existed was not news; the widespread range of it was—though in a strict sense this should not have been news either. It is impossible now to know just how long widespread extramarital sex has existed. For too long our moral code forbad the recognition, much less the circulation, of word about such a cancerous growth. Now that facts and figures, accurate or inaccurate, concerning all types of sex practice are out in the open, now that Dame Society has become more understanding and consequently more lenient about the whole subject of sex, we may well expect an increase of sexual freedom. However, no one in his right mind would suggest or expect sex without marriage to rival or supersede sex within marriage. Any thoughtful critic of our structure of ethics will turn his attention elsewhere when the individual's right to practice sex where, how, and with whom he likes is granted by law and accepted by convention. Thanks to Freud, Kinsey, et al, a good start has been made, and when that diehard, Organized Religion, is won over, when sexuality itself is no longer regarded by the church as a very dirty necessary evil instead of the fundamental drive it is, sex morality, as we now see it, can be deleted from the list of titillating controversial subjects. Then, perhaps, the idea of Sex Without Marriage will concern us far less than that other very grave and real problem, marriage without sex.

But what does sex without marriage mean anyway? The answer, broadly, is sexual freedom. It includes Sex Before Marriage, Sex After Marriage Is Ended, Sex Within Marriage, but shared with someone other than a legal mate, and Sex with a Partner of One's Own Choice. This latter stipulation would greatly ease the troubles of homosexuals, that poor harried and hunted lot, who because of an antique and cruel law must live a great part of their lives in the shadows.

HOPE IN THE HOPE CHEST

It is fairly safe to assume since so many people are married, or have been married, that people marry not only because it is the expected thing to do, but because they want to be married, or be in an equivalent relationship. The same thing is true about parenthood; in our society most of our birthrate is not the result of nature inexorably taking its course, but nature being *allowed* to take its course. Contraception is no enemy of parenthood; people still like to have babies and probably always will.

What then would the effect be on national life if society condoned the practice of sex without marriage? Judging from the results which have followed the amending or rescinding of other stern and unjust laws, written and unwritten, life would be easier. Relaxation is far more likely to produce well being than sloth. And just as divorce didn't put a stop to marriage and as contraception didn't bring an end to humanity, sexual freedom wouldn't wipe out the home and family as it exists today. Convention is fond of making deep frowns and dire predictions, but Convention is a little paranoid when it comes to feeling threatened, or as cowardly as the spoiled child who screams bloody murder at the mention of the word doctor. Conversely, for instance, did bundling render the Pennsylvania Dutch godless or increase the rate of illegitimacy?

If sexual freedom was one of our basic freedoms, a part of every child's heritage, a great many of our emotional disorders—disorders which cannot fail to affect our behavior in marriage and parenthood—would be alleviated. For an acceptance of sex as natural on all levels, a natural acceptance of it, would shrink the monster, now magnified out of all proportion, down to size; then it would dwell quietly along with its brothers, the other basic instincts. Now with its screaming zealots, its profaners, its apologists, and those whose obstinacy exceeds their wisdom when they all but deny its existence, the word sex itself almost automatically sets up an anxiety in all who hear it. Borne high above the heads of the noisy crowd, the subject is like a witch being carried to the stake. If and when people really do become sane and sensible about sex, the old saw about its "ugly head" will be utterly meaningless to those living after the Sexual Revolution. Together with cutting the beast down to size will go the impression that sex is not comely. This miracle of plastic surgery will be one of the finest operations that public opinion ever accomplished. And the national good health will prosper. While the Lone Wolverine may always be with us, the Bitch in Heat (her guilt about the sexual act undoubtedly starting in childhood when it was firmly stamped upon her conscience and unconscious that such a filthy thing was only tolerated in oder to produce babies) will not; instead she will make the good wife and mother that she thinks she is, but without her present distortion.

Sexual enlightenment has already accomplished a great deal toward restoring sexual health. An increasing number of men and women everywhere, in small towns as well as cities, not only find that non-married sex has lost its shock value, but fail to find "anything wrong" in it. Maybe they have always had this opinion, but until very recently it was one quietly held.

Literature and television too have helped enormously in cleaning the dirt off the subject of sex. Before mass market paperback books first appeared, just under twenty-five years ago, book censorship flourished, much embellished with asterisks, and of course called for the deletion of four-letter words relating to things sexual or scatological—for instance, a famous novel by E. E. Cummings, much prized by book collectors in its first edition, was recalled immediately after publication and painstakingly the word "shit" was blacked out by the publisher and his staff. Today, finding a copy of this book—THE ENORMOUS ROOM—with the word still intact, is quite a coup for the bibliophile. It was not long after paperbacks began to catch on that more and more publishers began reprinting semi-scholarly non-fiction, previously available and known only to students, colleagues and intellectuals. These books, works of sociologists, psychologists, anthropologists, historians and other scientists and scholars concerned with the human race and what it is, were, of course, filled to the brim with informed and detailed accounts and analyses covering every aspect of human thought, behavior and endeavor. While there was scant use of "dirty" words, (scholars know the technical ones as well) the knowledge so massively and coolly arrayed for mass public consumption dealt with every hush-hush subject under the sun. It was as if a giant named Science had stooped down, peered inside every window of every stained and grimy ivory tower of taboo, examined the contents and then gave his objective report. The towers began to crumble. Movie censorship was also lightened, and it seems hard to believe now that when Clark Gable as Rhett Butler in "Gone With the Wind" said, "Frankly, my dear, I don't give a damn" that silver screen history was made. The word damn reverberated throughout the world.

Television probably deserves more of the credit for cobweb cleaning of hush-hush subjects than it has as yet received. First, it gained its public by offering such placebos as shows starring already famous stars in the entertainment field, old movies, baseball, political events of national interest, prize fights, etc., but even at its begining TV boasted a good many programs of interest to thoughtful, enlightened people—programs far outnumbered, to be sure, by the sort of fare that caused television to be dubbed "The Idiot Box." And unfortunately it is true that most of the good early TV shows watched and admired by the well-informed have vanished—often to be replaced with a Western. But others have come into being, and the so-called popular shows, to be seen on nationwide networks have definitely broadened and liberalized their range of subject matter, even if the dramatic and literary quality is still doubtful. It is a laudable and almost unbelievable strike for the cause of enlightenment to know that a short time ago "The Defenders," a popular series on a nationwide hook-up presented a program on the subject of abortion, the treatment of which was not unrealistic and certainly not unsympathetic.

So, too, have books established their right to print words instead of asterisks, to walk freely and comment frankly in areas of human activity once posted to all but the grudgingly tolerated scholarly treatises. Since Mother Public finally took her dusty eyeglasses from the top of her head and caught on to the fact that serious novelists—not deliberate pornographers—never write smut for smuts sake, the four-letter word and the four-letter word situation appear quite unselfconsciously whenever needed. All over America, newsstands now sell such old maligned classics as LADY CHATTERLEY'S LOVER, THE BLACK BOOK, THE TROPIC OF CANCER.

Similarly, too, movies, better than ever or worse, have, at least, lost their squeamishness about portraying many important and revealing facets of "the facts of life." While the most controversial (read "shocking") have been foreign imports—"The Devil in the Flesh," Bardot's smash hits, "La Dolce Vita," "Les Liasons Dangereuses"—"Lolita" traveled to the screen here, altered from the book, but the intrinsic treatment of the subject—the message, too—weren't among the alterations.

While D. H. Lawrence might have been a little premature in 1917 at the exclamation which serves as a title for one of his books, LOOK! WE HAVE COME THROUGH, it took far less time for such a remark to be applicable than many discouraged lovers of human nature thought.

SEX AND THE LAW

Most people think that all sexual intercourse outside the legal married state is against the law, and is a Federal offense. As with most laws, most people simply don't know them. Law and sexual tolerance have a much closer connection than Society and sexual tolerance—a point very clearly indicated in that the general public believes non-marital sex to be a nationwide punishable crime. New York State, for instance, has no law against fornication when it means sexual intercourse engaged in by unmarried persons of legal age and of opposite sexes. Yet no unmarried couple can register under their own two names and occupy the same hotel room.

Federal law is broad indeed; the one outstanding law affecting sexual relations is the Mann Act, and this Act would appear to be largely a protective measure for state laws which do prohibit unmarried copulation.

Similarly, other SWM practices are under the jurisdiction of state law, rather than national, all of which indicates that Government, on the national level, is something of a wise, old and much maligned worldly owl. But wise old owls can also be sleepy ones, and cowardly ones. In order to bring practice and concept and justice together, the parental end of the government often must pinch itself awake and breast the tide of anger to over-rule the say-so of its underlings, or inequity and hardship result and continue to do so. Reviewing, if not out-and-out revision, of all state laws concerning sexual practice is much needed to help take up that slack called our cultural lag.

But if many state laws on the sex subject are as antequated as hoop skirts, and, indeed, date from their time, law on the state level too is often a lazybones and behaves like those cheerful little imps, the three optimistic monkeys who neither see, hear, nor speak evil. Of course, if the right spirits of ammonia are applied to the nose of Legal Lazybones, he sits up right away.

Such may account for the fact that the laws governing obscen-ity are disregaraded as wantonly in some areas as they are strictly enforced in others. Visitors returning from Pompeii (postcards of the ruins smuggled through) and from viewing the copula-tory sculptures of India and other places in the Far East, could find erotica and pornography abounding in their own country, and if under the counter at all, just under it. Of course, we do not have any great temple ruins of an erotic nature on display, but archaeologists of the future will find plenty of evidence that ours was a culture not disinterested in sex, however artless—and without art—the level. The on-the-market obscenities to be looked at and purchased now include not just the old scato-logical standbys—minature chamber pots, privies, etc., available in souvenir stores—but objects, usually considered "cute," that slyly suggest genitalia. A recent addition to the latter collection of wares was a pair of potholders, to be used by homemakers for removing hot pans from the stove, in the form of two sets of miniature Bermuda shorts in currently chic fabrics; upon closely examining these irresistibly adorable hostess gifts, the observer is rewarded to find that within a discreet opening in the crotch of each pair is a replica of male genitalia in one, and, in the other, representing, one assumes, female genitalia, a piece of brown fur masquerading as pubic hair! The female pudendum may be more difficult for time-conscious non Oriental craftsmen to duplicate, but the fact that no effort was made to do so, and that pubic hair alone seemed to serve the purpose perfectly well, is an interesting commentary on the creator of this giftware and on the public.

As much as such ignorance and vulgarity discredit progress in sexual freedom it still serves to indicate that some progress is there.

CHAPTER TEN

Among those who shook sorrowful wise heads at the future of human understanding and culture was Aldous Huxley. In an article called "Smoke" published in DECISION, a little magazine now as ancient and defunct as the early forties when it was born and died, Huxley held no hope for the success of mass culture or the elevation of mankind to enlightenment. It was his feeling that human beings would continue to stumble around down in their jungles of ignorance, and that in time the result of mass education would be an encroachment of the jungle itself, covering all culture, with only a slightly less dense and slightly shorter underbrush. Nothing, as it turns out, could be further from the truth. The national average I.Q. has risen several points in the last two decades, and the girl of twenty today, living in North Carolina, Texas, Wyoming or Delaware, is certainly better informed about the world at large, and more sophisticated about "culture" than Carol Kennicott would have been had she lived all of her life in New York, or some other dazzling throne of enlightenment.

Moreover, more people are going to church than ever before—a fact that would have caused the early H. L. Mencken disgruntled astonishment.

Consequently, perhaps it is only to be expected that people—particularly young people—throughout the land are beginning to find the whole subject of sex outside of marriage a tiresome one, and not nearly so important as all the attention that is paid to it and the trouble stirred up about it. One day, perhaps, the breath-catching question of "Should I, or should I not?" will seem as quaint, and rather cute, as the question that furrowed the noble ancestress' brow when she wondered if it wasn't downright wicked to show the tip of her shoe; or, even as late as the late thirties, when "nice" girls still worried about necking and petting. But while shoe tips are now the last thing a suitor would consider provocative, and necking and petting are simply accepted as what a girl does on a date with a man who interests and excites her, the question of having sexual intercourse with one's beau is still due to receive careful and serious consideration.

LADY IN WAITING

Undoubtedly, it is better to marry than to burn, but it would seem that another alternative or two might have been invented, or at least have come to notice, since that question was posed. While marriage may no longer be forever, as divorce and separation statistics indicate, most people who enter marriage do so with the desire to make it a permanent thing; not for convention's sake, but for their own. Consequently, the idea of getting married to control the fires of sexual desire seems absurd, unrealistic and downright dangerous. Meteorologists are better able to predict where lightning will strike than the professional expert on human behavior is in knowing who will be sexually attracted to whom. Educated guessing is as far as he will permit himself to go. Such affinities can be studied and understood to a certain degree after they happen—"She reminds him of his first sweetheart"— "His hands look like her father's," etc., etc.—but the next quill from the quiver may lodge in an entirely different spot and set up an entirely different set of clues for breaking down the equation; yet the white heat of passion may burn with exactly the same intensity and in precisely the same way. And being sexually smitten can happen again and again, almost countless times if the subject is willing for it to happen, throughout a lifetime—and, like lightning, it, too, sometimes does strike in the same place.

Therefore, few sensible people marry in order not to burn. The delicious swooning sensation when he touches you, the accelerated pulse, the divine glow, the bliss are not worth investing a married future in if everything else he thinks, says and does seems detestable. Such an intense sexual attraction to a person otherwise coldly disapproved of is, happily, rather extreme and therefore unusual. But it does happen. What then? Should Jane shake her head, admonish herself not to be such a fool as to involve herself with the likes of him? Or should she rationalize, bolstering temptation by remembering what Dorothy Parker said about sexual intercourse not constituting a social introduction? If she has any self-control (not pride; that's another thing entirely), she will cease and desist, for while sexual intercourse may not constitute a social introduction it often leads to one. Involvements have the insidious habit of growing in the dark, so to speak; they need far less care and nourishment than one might think. And even if Jane, sturdy of determination, decides to give that poor pleading body of hers just this one break, the chances are that poor, pleading body will greedily wheedle for more, or that the capricious organism, after the sexual overtures have passed and the mating act begun, decides when it is far too late and embarrassing to discontinue, that it wasn't so hot after all. Then Jane is left with the hardly comforting knowledge that she has just engaged in a one-night stand with a person she not only loathes but who doesn't even interest her physically.

A good rule of thumb for any woman who has the right or creates the right to make her own sexual decisions, is never engage in coition with a man you wouldn't like to know as a friend. Any compromise in this will result in unpleasant involvements—often torturously boring and time-waisting ones, if not hurtful as well—or a troop of fly-by-night one-night standers, odious after passion has been appeased, and about as meaningful to that marvelous and mysterious miracle of sexual intercourse as a Coca Cola is to thirst quenching—and far less pleasant, and probably far less satisfying.

If the sexual act were not such a many-splendored thing in its potentialities, and when, with the right partner, the four-letter word did not of its own accord magically transform itself and the act into love-making, misuse of sexual activities would not seem so coarse, vandalistic and profane. But sexual intercourse, as foolish and undignified and pointless as it may be, the act per se, is still capable of being the highest pleasure known to humanity, with a beauty so blindingly intense, so stirring, that no one who has ever written about it has been able to communicate more than a flicker of its ecstacy and essence. The man who wrote most successfully about it was Aristotle who, wisely, did not try to scale the heights, but instead deliberately stripped it of its elusive, intangible riches and, viewing it bare, marveled at the incredible fact that an act which in itself was so silly and insignificant could raise its performers to such pinnacles of rapture.

If one has no moral compunctions against participating in non-married sex relations, having one-night stands or brief affairs of no consequence usually bring about no serious psychic aftereffects. Or if guilt or shame exist at all, they are as emotionally unimportant as pique at oneself for overdoing self-indulgence; much the same kind of reaction a very popular girl might feel over the vast number of boys she has allowed to kiss her. And, too, there is that same kind of barely acknowledged, minute but nevertheless warm flame of self-satisfaction. Women, too, are pleased with their number of conquests, or with the number of men who have quested after them and who pleased enough not to be refused. However, for the woman who has loved deeply and who knows the depths of satisfaction and the heights of ecstacy of complete sexual union with her mate, casual affairs and ships that pass in the night seem pretty poor pickings indeed; she knows that to depend on them entirely is as pathetic as poverty. Consequently, she has only pity and compassion for The-Bitch-in-Heat woman who, in her frenzied sickness, trying male after male in an effort to appease her ravenous and hopeless hunger, can never experience orgasm and the profound peace and satiety that follow. She knows what Bach's music was saying in "O, Joy of Man's Desiring!"

The Lone Wolverine also knows what all the fuss is about. But the Lone Wolverine, being a gal with both heads on her shoulders, knows too that after the music dies the silence is deafening and unbearable and that there is a place for second best in any practical world. She is the kind of woman who has mellowed and who accepts compromise; she holds no bitterness. She considers herself lucky (as indeed she is) that she has gotten so much out of love, even though she now has no one to show for it. She is sorry that her particular character, her strength, her good sense and initiative and self-sufficiency unsuit her for any but a very rare kind of marriage to a very superior kind of man. But she knows, from very painful experience, that men who do not match her own qualifications resent her, and when they are mean, as well, inevitably pull the bullying act: either she is accused of "competing," trying to act and think like a man when she is only a weak, foolish little woman; or privately they size her up as an unconscious lesbian—or maybe even a conscious but cautious one! The Lone Wolverine is the kind of female who has heard herself contemptuously described as a woman with balls. And she is the kind of woman who is enormously pleased and gratified at the description. What could be better than having the best of both possible worlds?

But Jane is a lady in waiting, and while she has some qualities belonging to the Wolverine, and some belonging to the Bitch, she is unlike them in almost every way. To begin with, she is younger, is more average (normal), and has had only the most rudimentary sexual experience—it has not gone beyond rather extensive petting with the boy she went steady with in high school and didn't marry—not because she was so avid to come to the city and take a secretarial job which might in time lead to a fabulous career, but because she realized that she was in love with love, not him.

Since coming to the city, however, she has fallen in love, however briefly it lasted. She met him through one of her two roommates who share the apartment, and he simply swept her off her feet. He was everything she had ever dreamed of, but when he immediately began to pressure her about entering into a sexual relationship at once, she refused. His arguments were intelligent and persuasive; she admired them for their eloquence. And while she had to concede a few points here and there, she continued to refuse, explaining that she wasn't able to think straight; she needed time. Her head, as well as her eyes, felt stuffed up with stars. Everything had happened so fast; everything was so confusing. Then before she knew it, he was gone. Why? Had he been shooting her a line? Had he met someone else? Had there been someone else all along, many someone elses? Had he changed his mind? Why? Because she wouldn't permit him to be intimate with her sexually? Is that all he saw in girls? In her? Had her ignorance and shyness dampened his ardor? Did he now feel sorry for her? Was that why he cut it short? Would he ever come back? Would she and her pride let him? Would she say yes this time if he did? If she did say yes would she really mean it, or just do it in order to hold him? Would sex hold him? Did he have sex with every girl? Had he forgotten her? Had he left in disgust, anger, boredom? Had he left in romantic gallantry? Would he come back after he had given her a little time to think things over? If he came back and she did say yes, would he lose his respect for her? Was it wrong to have sex before marriage when the couple loved each other? Did he really love her? Would he love her more after sex? Less? Would she love him still after she gave in to him? Would she like it? Would it ruin her life or enrich it? Why was it so important anyway? Why couldn't he have waited a little? Why hadn't he once called her since? Did he think her stupid? Was she the only prude he'd ever met? Who did he think he was?

On and on and on.

Needless to say, he did not come back. Which was just as well for Jane, as her ardent young man, with all his charms and blandishments, and his whirlwind wooing, was already well on his way to follow in the steps of his master, Don Juan; before the year was out he had already met, won, and tired of at least ten others, though with each of the ten he had told himself—and the pursued—that this time was really it, and had meant it momentarily. But the experience for Jane had had its usefulness, for all the agony. The stars that had stuffed up her head, preventing her from doing the flash thinking and decision making he had wanted, all sadly tinkled down and broke on the floor when he left her, leaving her mind as clean and clear as a whistle, and as empty. Consequently, when all her doubts and questions began to crowd and shove into that vacant room, she found she could accommodate them all, and juggle them expertly.

After she had spent a few days absorbed in this and had gone as far toward understanding "everything" as she could go, the aching throb to bring him back to life through talking about him, at least, made her confide in her roommates. Not only did they

hear the whole story (which they already knew through conjec-
ture and observation), but Jane found, in hearing their interpre-
tations of his behavior, and confidences of their own regarding
similar unexplained misfortunes, that she understood more than
she thought she had; that many conclusions she had reached and
then rejected as being "too awful, too heartless," were right, sad
as the truth was, and she'd better take them back again. Also,
her curiosity about the whole question of sex before marriage
became even more stimulated as she and her friends talked.

Jane's roommates came from backgrounds much like her
own: small towns in rural communities, a little too far from
New York for the gloss to have rubbed off on the local culture or
for worldliness to have penetrated the cells of its mores; towns
where everybody went to church on Sundays and atheism was
thought to be a diabolical sort of Red Russian non-religion which
Khrushchev whipped his cowering (but innocent) slaves into
accepting. They all came from "nice" homes (not quite middle
class; none of their parents had college degrees, though Jane's
mother had gone to a state teachers' college for two years, long
enough to get her teaching certificate which had stood them in
good stead just after the war when she helped out her husband's
income by teaching third grade when he was trying to get started
in business); they had all loved high school—not just the social
life—and had been good, serious students, graduating near the
tops of their classes, yet very popular too. And they were all firm
in their minds about what they wanted out of life: a home, a good
husband, a family not just yet, but after a few years when they
would have accrued both experience in life (so they wouldn't
make mistakes in judgment) and business—for above all, they
wanted Security, and were willing to go on working after marriage in order to have it. Their ages, too, were close: they were
all in their early twenties; and while none were beauties, they all

had reasonably good figures and were frequently told they were "pretty." There the similarities stopped.

To Jane's vast astonishment, she learned that not only was she the only virgin, but both of her roommates had had extensive sexual experience—including a very serious, if not tragic, experience: one of her roommates had had a baby.

While Jane's own upbringing had not been exactly pious (her parents were Baptists), it had, in a way, been mealy-mouthed. Her only sex education from her mother (absolutely none from the father) had been in the way of correction, often enigmatic but very sharp and alarmed correction. It always happened, it seemed, when Jane was going about her own business, not thinking about anything in particular—dawdling. Then suddenly, for no reason at all, she would be shocked into awareness with her mother's imperious, "Stop that! Don't ever let me see you do that again!" "Stop what?" Jane had invariably asked in the beginning, but the question was just as invariably met with silence. So gradually she learned not to ask why and simply "stopped," with only the dimmest awareness of what she was stopping. In this way, she had learned that certain things were not "nice," a few of which made her blush to remember; they were things she had done that she almost consciously knew she had no business doing. For the more basic, the "raw" facts of life, she had had to depend on schoolmates—and, in one instance, on a teacher: her 7th grade science teacher—a man—had had to tell her about menstruation, this being necessary since it happened for the first time during his class. That was the day, feeling incurably wicked, she had first thought of and whispered under her breath a curse word—one intended for her mother. No "foul" language had ever been spoken at home.

Consequently, when her roommates calmly and openly began to talk about their sexual experiences, Jane literally gaped with astonishment. How could they have done such things? They *knew so* much; they were too young to know so much in the first place, and in the second, wasn't it pretty awful that they had done all this without at least being married? Then when Jane learned that one of the girls had actually had a baby—and deliberately out of wedlock; she had not "been in love with" the father, and besides, he was far too young to get married, as was she. Casually the girl went on to say that it had all worked out even better than she and her parents could have wished: a married, but childless first cousin of her mother's who lived in Detroit was only too glad to take the baby. She was crazy about kids, had been trying to have one for years, and she and her husband had almost decided to go to an adoption agency when this lucky accident came along.

Jane, of course, asked all the pertinent questions—at the same time fighting down physical nausea over the whole thing: hadn't her roommate "loved" the child? The roommate replied that he was "cute," but she had hardly gotten to know him—and oh, she'd see him sometime, she guessed. Weren't her parents horribly upset? Sure, they were, but they felt she had done the right thing. What about school—and all? Well, what *about* school? Well, nothing about school particularly. Only she had had to give up her drum majorette activities; too strenuous, and bad for the child....

After Jane had finished with her interrogation of the unwed mother, she was silent. It took her a long time to digest all that she had learned. It was quite bad enough, it seemed to her, that the other roommate had parted with her virginity at the age of fourteen—with the boy she had gone steady with from the time she was twelve and up to and including the present; the boy she would most likely eventually marry, though last year she had been crazy about another guy here in New York and had gone to bed with him—but hearing the details of pregnancy and the calmness with which everybody accepted it, deeply shocked Jane and somehow offended her. Later, however, she was able to analyze her displeasure: it was due to feeling as if someone had pulled something over on her; she had been taught—if not directly, but by strict implication—that parents severely punished daughters who came back from the primrose path with a pocket full of posies, so to speak; that the boy should have been forced to marry her, love or no love, or sent to reform school; and, finally, that society *never* countenanced such things, even if God in his Heaven could forgive such sin. That all concerned—even her teachers and the townspeople—had behaved naturally and sanely, struck Jane not just as fantastic, but somehow remiss. The girl *ought* to have been punished. Then she had to ask herself: But why? Wasn't it punishment enough that the girl had had to suffer the discomforts of pregnancy, the pangs of birth, all for a child she hadn't the faintest desire to bear and be held accountable for? Then Jane decided yes, and took pleasure from the fact that for once the irony of fate had been reduced to harmless dust.

SEX AND DECENCY

The story of Jane's roommate actually happened, just a few years ago, and the details are accurate. The small town in which the girl lived was the usual small town; it had its typical, mean gossips, its pseudo-pious, unforgiving narrow-minded people with a scattering of wise and well-read others; it had its small town smugness. In short, for a novelist, it would have seemed the perfect spot to select as a setting for a story about slander and how it can ruin lives. Why didn't it ruin this girl's life? Who can tell. Perhaps it would have slowly, creepingly squeezed the life out of her had she not left immediately after graduating from high school. But while she was in high school—and the amazing thing is that the entire faculty were in agreement that she should stay—she was as popular and as sought after as ever, by girls and boys alike—even though she was attending classes with her growing belly under maternity clothes! There were, of course, a few grumblings, mostly from parents of her schoolmates about how it was outrageous, indecent, etc., but no one had the nerve, not even in meetings of the P.T.A. to protest against her liberal treatment! Her parents, his parents, their friends, their teachers won their position, it would appear, by simply brazening it out! Of course such sane, levelheaded averting of tragedy may never happen again in years, if at all. But the point is it *did* happen! Which proves that human beings, ignorant, biased human beings, can rise above their own hypocracies and prejudices when they have a choice between saving something so invaluable as another's destiny or destroying it.

The girl was fortunate, too, in her own wisdom, as well as her remarkable good luck and good parents. It would have been a fatal error to have effected a marriage between two fifteen-year-olds simply to legitimatize a child which was a pure act of nature, and nothing more. Similarly, it would have been downright medieval to send the boy off to reform school (why not the girl too?) where he would become embittered, possibly corrupted into criminality. Instead, both youthful parents probably learned a most profound lesson: illicit liasons, unless entered with some due precaution, however casually entered, can have resounding, almost never-ending tragic effects. They all learned this, but they did not have to stay chained to their punishment, listening to the resounding like a gong in their ears, throughout their particular eternities.

And what of Jane, and the effect of all this sordid knowledge poured into her innocent ears? Jane, being a practical, good-natured, kindly girl with a fairly good mind, could not have heard any sexual accounts which could have profited her more; nor vicariously experienced sex from a better source. Too inhibited sexually herself, by her own inhibited, sheep-minded parents, she might have gone for years torturing herself with sex guilt, clinging to virginity as fiercely as if it were a thin coat in a blizzard, then parting with her maidenhood at last with some person as sick and as caddish as her first would-be lover, or romantically saving herself for her husband—a person who would probably be a far cry from her "ideal"—and then being disappointed in the whole thing—all this if she had not had that particular set of roommates who, inadvertently, provided her with an excellent foundation for a working knowledge of sex. Moreover, to answer her further questions—to give her accurate details—after explaining as simply and as casually as they could what sex was "like," they referred her to several excellent books in the field—at least two written from diametrically opposed viewpoints—so that she could compare what they had said with the clinical findings and opinions of experts and make up her own mind where she personally stood on Sex Without Marriage.

In time, Jane took a lover, a man some five years older than she, whom she was fond of, attracted to, but not in love with. This man, who was a person altogether worthy of Jane's interest and affection, supplemented—or bore out—Jane's own convictions about what sex is, what it isn't, what it should be and what it shouldn't be. He taught her, among other things, that sexual dishonesty—primarily self-dishonesty, cowardice, self-doubt—was the cardinal, and possibly the only, bedroom sin, to be followed closely by the egregious practice of substituting euphemisms for "strong words that don't sound nice even if they are in the dictionary and doctors use them," and mistaking inhibition for good manners. "Good manners in the bedroom are the same as good manners everywhere," he said. "Behaving as naturally as possible and at the same time being considerate of others."

Jane was rather sorry she hadn't fallen in love with him, but he hadn't fallen in love with her either. She remained just romantic enough to want to be in love with the man she married. But who would he be, and where was the best place to meet him?

MEN: WHO, WHAT, WHERE, WHEN?
OR SEX *WITH* MARRIAGE

Caitlin Thomas wrote a scathing diatribe against men in the form of an open letter to her teenage daughter which was recently published in HARPER'S magazine. Venom dripping from every fang, she proceeded to list, describe and size up all the types young Miss Thomas was likely to meet and what she, Mama, personally thought of such types and her experience with them. One can only say that Dylan Thomas couldn't have been all *that* bad a husband, and to hope that his daughter is in for as many pleasant surprises as her mother has met with unpleasant ones.

Agreeing with Mrs. Thomas, men *are* rather awful, but so are women, and that's that. Anyway, people are all we have to work with and we might as well get used to them. Always, when giving any thought to the subject of the husband potential, the temptation is to write down the word "None" and forget about it. But it isn't true. It isn't true in Goodnight, Kentucky; and isn't true in Nome, Alaska; it isn't true for Alice Blue Gown, age 18, and it isn't true for Mrs. D. A. Revolution, age 69, or in all the towns and cities and girls (an American woman is a girl until she dies) in between. Them as wants gets.

But what is there to want and where to get?

There being a slight plethora of women around doesn't help, of course, but there are still plenty of would-be husbands just waiting to be plucked off by the right hand. Needless to say, the husband-to-be crop is only a bumper crop during war years, and in numerical distribution, in any year, if put all together they would form the most interesting, tallest, exciting (to say nothing of uncomfortable) pyramid ever built! In other words, Alice has millions to choose from, while Mrs. R. has only thousands (and then she might have to commit a little sorocide) at best. Also, when thinking about marriage with no husband in sight, the would-be bride is limited by her location and her own aims, unless she is prepared to change both.

For the girl living in a small town, if, by the time she is 25 and has looked the local bunch over, or been overlooked (which can also happen, and does more often than not), her prospects for meeting and marrying anybody locally are slim as a snake and exactly as heartwarming. The best that can happen is 1) she will have second-sights about the boy next door 2) somebody will die (female, of course) 3) that dashing new man at the plant will pick *her* out at the annual Wallflower's Ball and forget all about those 66 others who have been chasing him like foxhounds 4) while visiting Sister Mary for the weekend in Chicago, Mr. Him will take one look at her and change into Instant Husband 5) the little boy next door won't seem so little any more 6) that the small disagreement Agnes had with that yummy husband of hers about who bent the Canasta card will definitely lead to divorce.

These are about the only local husband-hopes Miss 2,000 to 10,000 pop. can entertain without leaving home to find more. And her 10,000 to 30,000 neighbor doesn't have it much better, either—adding the number "five," along with the proper plural endings, to each of the chances on the foregoing list just about does it. Except, of course, in towns and small cities near army posts and such, or where large plants, branches of national industries, are located; here the turnover is usually not inconsiderable, and there still are *some* bachelors, or some who will be again!

As for bigger cities, the metropolises, there are men, men, men; professional men, businessmen, laboring men, postmen— and probably even some cave men, if that is the heart's desire. But the catch here is that the catch in the net is going to be meagre, even scraping the bottom, for the waters are well fished. Girls simply pore into cities in search of husbands, settling quietly down in offices usually until they get a strike. But they are to be had if the girl is patient, pretty and poised enough. The worst mistake is giving up too soon, or going slightly berserk at the sight of all that competition and snapping up some marked-down thing off the bargain counter just so as not to go off empty handed. Among the items *not* to look for (and this applies particularly to husband shoppers in the 30-40 plus age group):

1) Any multi-married man between marriages. Chances are he is between divorces, not marriages. The more often he has married, the less likely he is as solid husband material.

2) The irresistibly credentialed, fairly attractive, well-to-do man whose one marriage ended fifteen years ago. That's right; his one marriage ended fifteen years ago.

3) The bottle babies. Lovable though they are, their growth is definitely stunted, and their knowledge of how to shrink others to size is as keen and extensive as a Japanese dwarf tree grower's. This is an underlined *not*. Not even for the girl whose ambition is to be president of A.A.

4) The man with a question mark invariably present after the word "man" unless the prospective fiancee regards sex and Napoleon brandy the same way: special occasions only. Not even if he *does* say how much he wants a son.

The wives of such son fanciers usually end up hating all homosexuals, and that's not fair.

5) The bachelor over thirty who lives at home. Make no mistake about it. That's where he wants to live. That second weaning makes him very fretful and everybody cross. (If not homo- and/or sui-cidal)

6) Starving artists. Reverse the two words for a forecast of the bride's future. If food is no object or if the girl is an eager, sturdy work-mare type, preferring treadmills to canters in the park, body and soul can be kept apart. But there has to be an awful heap of togetherness to keep love from becoming stuck-togetherness.

7) The Gay Blade. Just what it says. He may shine very handsomely, but a blade is still a knife. Better for throwing than handling.

8) The octogenarian worth a million bucks. When the beady little eyes light up and the claw extends the three-carat diamond which belonged to his second wife, the smart girl asks him how much will be her salary. Chances are that the three-carat diamond *still* belongs to his second wife, or at least to her heirs, who, it will develop, are buzzing around like flies at a picnic in an open-air pavilion. The bird who enters such a gilded cage will never forget the sound of that gate slamming—both when she's shown in and after the funeral when she's thrown out.

... And lots more. This doesn't mean that 1,2,3,4,5,6,7, & 8 will go begging. *Anybody* can get married who is of a mind to. But it does mean that any girl who deliberately chooses anything from one through eight inclusive had better fasten her seat belt because it is going to be a rough trip. Marriage is no joy ride in any case; it's a long, exhausting journey with all the pleasures, annoyances, excitements and boredoms of a journey, and a lot more besides. So much for the lists of don't's. Here is a list of do's—necessarily drawn in outline only:

Do

Marry before thirty, if possible. A wife who enters marriage at a later age feels in a rush to have children while she's still young and to save them from the fate of having old parents. A wife will need all of her brightness and energies to devote to her marriage and to settling into her home the first few years, and in her twenties she can afford them.

Marry for love, but don't close the door there. Make sure that like and respect get in too. And, ideally, mutual interests, shared opinions (at least on a few major subjects like religion and children), similar education and background should be included. Naturally, sex is counted in under the "mutual interests" heading.

Choose someone whose age is not incompatible now or in the years of middle age. It may be all very well for a woman to marry a man ten years younger than she, but when she's 50 he will be 40—the rarin'-to-go age for everything this side of the animal kingdom! The same thing is conversely true for a woman who marries a man older than she, only the limits for this age difference is more like 15 years instead of 10. (Men fancy that they stay young and attractive longer. Maybe they do.) The ideal age difference between husband and wife is 2 to 7 years, so that they are contemporaries, but vast age differences—20 years and up—have occurred between many, many happy wives and husbands.

Take the in-law jokes seriously. The woman who doesn't like her husband's family and vice versa, or friends, and again vice versa—scramble it up any which way and the problem still comes out the same—(or he hers) had better plan to set up housekeeping in a rocket headed for the moon. For while disagreement about friends and family isn't a major cause for divorce, it *has* been known to cause divorce, and in any event it is pretty grim.

This next Do may seem like quibbling, but *Craig's Wife* would understand:

Give him the toothpaste test before the wedding day. A great many slobs are women, but here, at least, men seem to have the numerical edge on them. And that tired old explanation about their mothers in hand-and-foot attendance doesn't quite account for it. If, in her beautiful, shining, neat bathroom, he leaves the top off the toothpaste and smears it and everything else in sight around into a Black-Sambo-and-the-Tiger non-confection—or if *she* does this to his—Stormy Weather! Whether *he* does, or whether *she* does, both will have to get used to it, for strongly compulsive people—in either direction—do *not* change. It is to be hoped that neither is very sloppy nor very orderly, on the other hand, but if one is and one isn't the twain are often going to wish they'd never met. Further, mutual habits in all areas tend to make marriage more comfortable. That old word "helpmate" goes back to the Bible.

And now for toting up the bill of particulars:

Remember that ad for traveler's checks which advises against carrying more cash than the carrier can afford to lose? The bride with *lots* of money is a special case and she probably has had the whole thing worked out in her head since it wore ribbon-bows, but the girl with *some* money—from a two-dollar bill to twenty thousand—had better give the matter plenty of forethought, or there will be plenty of afterthought, probably accompanied by looks that could kill. Say the bride has worked for a few years and has saved some, say the bride inherited it or received it as a gift from her parents or other relatives (this does not include those checks people give as wedding presents), the question is: Is it hers after the honeymoon is over, or is it his? One thing is sure: it can never be *theirs*, even if Himself later on doesn't make that slip about his wife having put up the downpayment on the house; it can never be *theirs* even if careful etiquette keeps both calling it that, and certainly despite the fact that they will probably both benefit from it. If a bride is sensible—and unselfish—she will part with her nest egg forever on the same day she parts with her maiden name; this is logical since the groom will probably assume the administration of their finances. Of course, if she has some personal reason for hanging on to her worldly goods, such as having promised to help little Billy through college, etc., she should. However, if she intends to add her share to the pot, she should add it and forget it—regardless of how the money is ultimately spent, or misspent. Any money she earns or inherits in the future, or any her spouse gives her, is another matter entirely. It's the initial offering that counts, and as the sum goes up (or really far down) it counts even more. Many a middle-aged family standby in the wrangle department has been about how John Doe lost Mary Doe's money; it seems like only yesterday. So, if Mrs. John Doe, Jr. wants to avoid this fascinating, convoluted grudge (there will be plenty of other topics available later on), she will casually hand him her check for deposit in their brand new joint account and forget she ever had it so good. If *he* wants to remember, let him.

As for that two-dollar bill—two-dollar bills are supposed to be terribly unlucky, and the bride who only has one to her name is terribly unlucky indeed, and will be more so if she has handed it to the kind of husband who will never let her forget the paltriness of the amount. And there are such bastards, unfortunately.

SAFETY IN NUMBERS

Husband-hunting and job-hunting have a lot in common: usually at the end, two or three offers come up at once; and the whole thing seems like a short breeze after the mission is accomplished. Also, like job-hunting, there is just so much time and worry and no more to devote to it, and just so many openings.

Most husband-hunting, however, is not done consciously. If, like Jane, the future-bride is reasonably happy, well-adjusted to her life & times, her friends and her sexual barometer is steady, the time spent as Lady in Waiting is one of the best of her life. If the pre-marriage girl is a city girl, there are endless diversions and endless people for her. If she is new in town and wants to give it a close look, the local library or a book store is sure to have a good collection of books on the city's lore, hiways and byways, restaurant tips, etc. But if she is all settled in and already *knows* that, believe it or not, West 11th Street intersects West 4th Street (Greenwich Village in New York), she probably knows exactly what to do with her spare time, and who to spend it with. The trouble often is—especially in a large city—that an attractive, unattached female will, after a time, have not just a circle of friends, but so many circles of them that she is literally running around in them trying to decide who, what, where, when and how. Of course, a lot of names in almost any well-filled address book must be counted as "don't counts"; such almost extinct, seldom referred to fossils as Mother's best school chum, or dead wood like The One That Got Away but still calls up occasionally and wonders why you don't come out to Westchester ever because Sue is *still* dying to meet you, and you should see the kids.

Also in the address book are quite a number of names of men who call occasionally, of which few are chosen. Rightfully, these demi-suitors qualify for the *not*-to-consider-for-marriage honor roll if the interested party is a stickler for keeping everything (and everybody) in its place, but though this is a suspect list, it could change any day into a "spec" list, and besides, these types are nice to keep around as pets (and very glamorous ones too!)

1) Airplane pilots (and almost all of the traveling species from river-boat captains to Fuller Brush salesmen). They are up in the air too much of the time, and anyway the airplane hasn't been perfected yet. Widow's weeds, however becoming, are Non-U.

2) Married men—all; be they doctor, lawyer, merchant, chief.

3) Visitors from the Mysterious East, West, all points north and otherwise. These present the same disadvantages as the boys on the road, except more so. Invariably, they all seem to come from impossible places where any bride in her right mind would literally have to be carried over the threshold, hog-tied and bound, to get her there at all. However, there are such things as transfers, and there are such places to shift to (or hail from) as Paris.

4) Free-lancing Anything. Again, doctor, lawyer, merchant, chief, or starting at the head of the jingle is more like it: rich man, poor man—a very good likeness of the groom. As a matter of fact, any man of gelatinous financial substance. He may be very nice to visit, but nobody to live with. Better to let him make his mark first, or it may get branded on the bride, spelling out in bold type: H-E-X.

Certainly these gentlemen belong in a Sex-Without-Marriage book, and would probably, at this tallying, sneak themselves in if it hadn't been done for them. In all fairness, the list could just as well be entitled "Potential Lovers," because for the most part, most men in any of the four categories have a great deal to offer vertically, sight unseen, which must of necessity be Position

Number One. (If they arrive in Position Number Two remove from Potential list and call ambulance.) Pilots are notorious euphorics, and in their hands money turns liquid. To a lesser extent, this is true of any of the others in the nomad classification, depending on the nature of their traveling. The Shanks' mare variety is the exception; unless he is the boss' son and happens to be walking his way up.

As for married men—explanation self evident. All the Lady in Waiting is likely to meet are just dying for a home away from home, even if it's just for an occasional drink before catching the 6:17. And who knows? Sometimes they miss the train. And sometimes they never even board it again. Somebody else's husband can be as cozy and safe as an old slipper—one capable too, if the stars and temperature are right, of being transformed into Prince Charming, no Fairy Godmother needed. But the magic won't work unless, prone or con, the magician remembers at all times that he is really somebody else's old slipper—not hers. That is, not until the divorce decree is granted and the shoe is on another foot.

The Visitors from a smaller planet or a larger, or this one, are the most likely candidates for moving up to a higher rating on a highly civilized civil list. Usually, any who have landed in the address book, or lodged in the mind, have passed muster with such vivid and splendid flying colors that it is with regret that they must be held back from the sanctum sanctorum where the names of the loved ones—quick & dead—are kept cushioned on velvet. But they are nomads too, long-shot commuters, and as long as they remain so (without making firm concessions as well as offers) the well-canned lass with can (see Chaucer) will intermittently suspend them from the Bridge of Sighs. Which, having saved the best for last, concerns that amorphous, variegated lot of Lancelots, the free-lancers:

These men are usually as bold, spirited, and as individualistic as their over-all classification would imply, and though less likely to succeed as candidates for the Sure Thing Husband Material group than the out-of-towners, for instance, they can do a lot to enrich the life of any Lady in Waiting. Moreover, some of them *do* succeed in a big way (for themselves and for the prospect list). Of course, the mere fact that they choose to go it on their own, instead of from 9 to 5 for somebody else, makes them very open to question: aren't they any good? Can't they get along with normal folk? Are they too far out?

Whether they are far out or far in, the ranks of the free-lancers do include some very superior, very diverting, very talented *mensch*. Aside from the possibility that he may write that hit play, win fame and fortune as a composer, or end up as the inventor of the atomic mousetrap, the free-lancer, his time being his own, is a very useful man to know in case of such emergencies as moving day, short circuits, burglars under the bed, etc.

WHERE THE BOYS ARE: CINCINNATI, SOUTH AMERICA, WAY OUT WEST, ALASKA AND OVERSEAS

For the girl who has said, "To hell with it!" in reference to Sex Without Marriage, whether she has been there or not, the crystal globe can hold only two futures: legally mated, or quite legal but unmated. If local resources have been exhausted for that Miss who has tried everything but a divining rod to locate the means of changing her name to Mrs., then something's got to give— namely, Miss. First, of a pocketful of trainfare, and, second, of her best. And if she wants to secure her investment, she will make herself as sharp as a ferret's eye and a serpent's tongue. If she is pulling out of New York City for any of the destinations listed in the heading, she will do well to: 1) pretend our Nation's

Capitol, Washington, D. C., is a ghost town, when and if she passes through (it is, as far as the husband mart is concerned. 2) leave, bridges bare but unburned, loaded—with money, clothes, determination, and everything but alcohol; first stop stateside: Cincinnati.

This is a recommended center for husband-getting, escort-getting, or just getting because it has begun catering to runaway white slaves, as opposed to its pre- and post-Civil War fame days when it was practically the first stop for Negroes on the underground railway run. Because of recent population growth, due primarily to the influx of big industry and the across-the-river gambling attractions in Kentucky (now at a standstill), this comparatively small city has found itself, in the last ten years, to be as fat and sprawling as a middleaged squire—and, still, full of hospitality, joie de vivre and largesse, and as ignorant as a backward country squire concerning what to do with the wealth. (It will learn—or has already.) Cincinnati is ripe for the picking—and the pickings are good. Any woman under forty who wants to get married stands as good a chance of not being turned away empty-fingered as her pioneer ancestress did when braving the Far West more than a hundred years ago.

As for the Far West, a lot of people gave up; and those wide open spaces, where pioneer braves were once dots, are wider and emptier than ever; very few dots to dot. And they are needed. And wanted. If the Waiting Lady has resolved to wait no more, if she is ox-strong, intrepid, fixated (single-minded), then let her take to the plains and the Painted Desert. She will be welcome, with or without covered wagon, if she can really take it.

As strenuous and challenging for all but ice babies, is our slice of frozen north, the new state of Alaska. Its manpower supply is famous, and thanks to industry, armed forces, etc., it's all true too.

To go to the other extreme, South America can boast a lot of merchandise on the husband mart; plenty of Americans are available as well as the well-known Latin lovers.

But overseas is the ideal combination of business with pleasure. If she can qualify for a government job, or can afford to take off on a traveling year, not only will the husband-prospector see a lot of marvelous sights, but will meet a lot of marvelous people. Marvelous people have a way of knowing other marvelous people, and some of them are sure to be eligible men. In short, any woman who is really determined to get married can do so, but any person of determination knows that it is much more than a five-syllable word.

So much for *where they are* and *who they aren't* tips for the determined. Who *is* good husband material, here, there and everywhere? Though wanting to get married is, in itself, no recommendation for husbandhood, it certainly doesn't hurt. Winning him over may be more fun than skittles, but it can be strenuous exercise and hard on the heart. Therefore, it is preferable if he is at least open-minded.

Also, he should be as interested in the DO MARRY list of recommendations as should his bride. Which means anything which has to be caught with a net may turn out to be about as useful for human husbandry as a butterfly. He has to be amenable to the prospect of maturity and eventually settling down, without the aid of formaldehyde, or stronger waters. He has to be interested in women as people, not just playmates, and in knowing them from all sides.

In short, any man who is available, is capable of supplying more than starvation rations and is proving it, who is not averse to taking a woman to wife on a serious basis—not just for kicks, or wheel here we go again—and is reasonably hale, hearty and reasonable is good husband material. Outside of that he can be anything from Tarzan to Tiny Tim, from Li'l Abner to Absent-minded Professor. Size, beauty, brains, occupation, opulence, and personality quirks are all relative, and she that would a-briding go should free herself of all prefixed absolutes after she has informed herself of her own intentions, pretensions and where the pitfalls lie which would in her own personal case most assuredly prove to be pratfalls. Rules, after all, were made to be broken, but not until the would-be breaker has memorized them first. Then comes the time to pick and choose.

LOOKING THE PART

If a girl wants to be a radiant bride, she must look like one first. Anybody with dead, mossy hair (however groomed), and lifeless, sallow complexion (this applies from stem to stern), no matter how stunning and expensive the chic little suit she is wearing, or how expert the makeup job, is little more delectable than a corpse. Unless it's the local mortician she has in mind, she had better start fixing up the inside first and go back to the outside later. This means, of course, good health.

It's true that Elizabeth Barrett got Robert Browning, but sickness—even if it's just frailty and anemia—is seldom interesting except to the sufferer, and seldom appealing except to the sympathies. Though the first erogenous zone may be the mind, as Delmore Schwartz has written, most would-be suitors in good health, poets notwithstanding, would find that elevator of emotion stalled right there on the top floor when encountering an attractive girl in a fainting fit. Perhaps this was not true in Great-Grandmother's time when every girl had her smelling salts, but medical science has vastly improved the national health since then, and ill health is no more the order of our day than it is an asset.

Vitamins having more or less replaced the apple-a-day (and much more convenient to carry around), and having greatly increased the vigor and vitality of the public at large, it seems rather astonishing that our hospitals manage to stay so full. The fact that they do, despite what the medical profession has discovered about sickness and health, would indicate that something or other has been lost in the shuffle. The something or other is, in all likelihood, the apple; or, more generally, all the food that we eat. Vitamins are supplements to nutrition, not nutrition. What we eat is what we are, and if it is dry toast, vitamins, dexedrine and black coffee, then that's it. Doesn't sound very tasty.

If the health is good, so, too, normally, is the figure. Consequently, dieting is seldom the problem of the woman who first of all understands diet. The best authorities seem to concur that a high protein diet is the most desirable, and if one can tell a protein from a carbohydrate there is no need to learn how to spell calorie.

It's as simple as that, and aside from that yearly routine checkup that every realistic person makes, chances are that the only time the doctor has to be called in is when he is needed as a fourth at bridge.

Bridge is good exercise for the brain, but, being a game, not a sport, it doesn't do anything particularly worthwhile for the body. The human body, if in good health, craves exercise as well as good food, and it should get it. If pedaling through the park is out of the question, push-ups will do. With exercise it isn't a question of where or even how, but when. Or, don't just *sit* there, for God's sake! A few minutes each day will take care of the problem of exercise for most people, and there are hundreds of very simple ones to choose from. The subject of exercise having been on the public bulletin board so long, almost everyone knows dozens already and has no need for consulting a book.

Once the body is fit, then it becomes important that the clothes fit the body. This means several things: that clothing should conform to the figure in the proper places and not be too big or too small; that it be appropriate to the occasion; and that the style be appropriate to the wearer, an extension of her personality as well an adornment of it.

As for the question of good taste, there is no excuse for having any other kind, fashion media being as copious and available as it is; there is merely an explanation: the badly dressed woman just doesn't care. But since most men *do* care if women aren't attired properly, and since most women care about men, female indifference to clothes is self-defeating, to say the least.

Also, and especially for the city woman, bank balance can no longer be the decisive factor in dressing well. A large clothes budget can determine quality and quantity and range of apparel in milady's wardrobe, but not taste, style, or attractiveness. With the nationwide increase in discount stores, factory outlets, etc., clothes not only are better than ever, but cheaper.

The smart New Yorker, for instance, not only has the advantage of such stores, but if she is sick of the "slightly irregulars," stylish or not, to be found in Klein's and Orbach's, and tired of wearing superior couturier numbers grabbed off at a ridiculous price, but with the labels snipped out, her heart's balm can still be easily restored—and for the same low price. Label-lovers, models, and thrifty millionairesses regularly patronize New York's thrift shops, some dozen of which are fabulous indeed, Mr. Michael's and Encore being among them. Here Diors, Balenciagas, etc., blossom as nonchalantly as orchids in South America, and the prices aren't hothouse either.

However, no Dior original is going to do very much for its wearer if she is unconcerned about what an earlier generation used to refer to as "daintiness." *Do* heed the TV commericals about deodorants and shampoos and soaps, and if the prices have gone up with the neighborhood *blanchisseuse,* there's always the laundromat; or if it has to be done by hand, it's a good way to keep fingernails clean.

THE MATING CALL, LOUD AND SOFT

Who sounds it, and at what pitch, *is* important, but not so important as knowing how to give it at all, or knowing how to detect it when it is given. Many a woman has mistaken a come-on as a brush-off, just as men very frequently make the same mistake in reverse. Therefore, people-study is to the human jungle what bird-watching is to the forest, if one is interested in such fauna. And she who looks like a radiant bride may never be one if she is also the dumb blonde.

Since science has not yet come up with anything in tablet form that will correct congenital imbecility, it would be imbecilic of a female on this level of the I.Q. scale to read this section of the book. But, as stated earlier, it has been observed that the national I.Q. average is on the rise, and the mental age of the majority is sufficient to enable them to become reasonably well-informed, thinking people.

Stupidity, or what appears to be, is very ofen not true incapacity to learn, but inability to concentrate. Fortunately, ability to concentrate can be developed, but not before the causes for the lack are removed. Mind-wandering, mental inertia, absentmindedness etcetera etcetera all indicate anxiety or emotional disturbance, and, unfortunately, belong to man's fate. But the mentally robust man or woman is not chronically given to these states, just as the well-adjusted person is not constantly beset with self-absorption and/or selfishness. The so-called "dumb blonde" then is usually a very selfish person though not necessarily an organically stupid one. Highly intelligent people and well-adjusted people usually know what they see and say and respond and react to what they hear and think. If they have their wits about them and are observing as closely as possible what goes on, their judgments are usually as sharp and as accurate as their emotional equipment will permit them to be. Also, the memory stores up all manner of things which in some people it unloads as perceptiveness.

Provided she is not full of neurotic insecurity about herself, no alert, attractive woman of reasonable intelligence should fail to perceive the difference between a man's interest and disinterest. If she does, it is because she is either not interested herself or hasn't been paying enough attention to the play. Ego, that great block and tackle, can be a great enemy as well as a friend to romance. Keeping it in its place is the secret.

When Jane was giving herself the third degree about why her young man walked out on her, her ego was acting up. Granted that ignorance (inexperience) got her into the involvement in the first place, and granted, too, that ego's following that particular piper was a quite natural thing, it was ego that fell and caused temporary blindness. For in the period Jane knew this young man, her mind quickly observed and absorbed facts which ego withheld from judgment. That she knew what he really was became apparent when ego at last admitted defeat.

NEVER SPEAK TO STRANGERS

This is all very well for children, but it is downright silly for a female adult, and a precautionary measure to be left behind for the well-mannered children who speak only when spoken to.

For a woman on her own, bent or not upon staying that way, speaking to strangers is essential—and inevitable if she has the

power of speech! Traveling in a foreign country without knowing one word of its language gives an indication of just how
impossible and ludicrous that nursery vestige is. Also, while the
mating call may be delivered in a number of ways other than by
word of mouth, relying upon the smile, the touch of the hand,
the flicker of an eye to turn the trick would be constraining; and
anything constraining, when getting across the message of love,
so to speak, is a mistake. Part of the joy of flirtation is its opening
moment of spontaneity.

The fascinator and the hard-sell sex salesman are one and
the same thing. Both are brassy, specious as a sideshow, and
usually as tawdry and disappointing ... providing they ever
deliver. But most such sex-appeal flaunters are all bark and no
bite. Fortunately, except for the naive or debauched (the latter
can always handle them) they seldom find any takers. Most of
the subjects they fasten upon for hawking their wares are suf-
ficiently sensitive and intelligent to find them embarrassing
and disgusting. Such mating calls can definitely be classified
under *loud*. This incidentally, is in no way connected with, or is
a criticism of that fine and admirable old custom of the Direct
Approach. The direct approach is beyond reproach: it is honest,
usually spontaneous, and, like any true work of art, without the
slightest trace of vulgarity. This call can be delivered at any volume, timbre, or pitch; it's up to the caller.

The minx, the coquette, the enchantress, the born flirt, etc.,
all first cousins, by the way, to the hard-sell sex duo, but more
gently bred, are well worth watching in action. Especially can
the lass whose mating call falls on deaf ears, if any, learn something from these charmers. One of the first things she is likely
to learn is that availability is not enough. There has to be some
animation too. She will observe also that a cavewoman bellow
may be effective here, but not there; style, like timing, has to be

adjusted to each subject, as does whether to play it cool or play it hot, and whether playing to a large audience or an audience of one. In the main, the successful flirt is so for these reasons: she is a quick study, she speaks well, and often wittily, she listens well and responds alertly, she appears even-tempered and as if she is enjoying herself (whether she is or not) and never upstages her partner. In short, many of the rules of the coquette game are the rules of the stage. This is a girl who knows how to say yes and mean no—even more important than the other way around.

PROTOCOL FOR SEX WITHOUT MARRIAGE

However, suppose this amatory thespian has said no and means yes, and gets around to proving it. What then?

One of the best cases for SWM is presented in Albert Ellis' chapter on premarital sex in his book SEX WITHOUT GUILT, and the title of the book itself is most significant. One of the first entries in any handbook of non-married sexual etiquette and conduct should be sex without guilt. If there is going to be guilt, there might as well be no sex. Guilt, like Asian flu, is very catching, though it may be a lighter case or mistaken for something else. But, whatever, it will not be pleasant—no more so than is sexual intercourse when one has a miserable cold, complete with sneezes, coughs, aches and pains.

The next rule in the codex is closely related to sex without guilt, and could serve as a subheading: fornication is fun. Agreed, this sounds more like a motto for a sampler than a rule, or a bill of goods to be used by the enticer on self or victim. (As a matter of fact it might not be a bad idea to work up into a sampler and hung above the nuptial bed.) However, whether the phrase is embroidered, written or unwritten, it must be brought to mind prior to sexual encounter. If it produces a grimace instead of a misty-eyed expression and a sigh, then, for some reason it is not in this particular case, or at this particular moment, true and discarding the project is the best idea. Sexual engagement should never be made as an accommodation, or to keep one's promise, and this is just as true in legal marriage as in SWM, though admittedly more difficult to enforce. However, the girl having the affair as opposed to the wife fulfilling her wifely duties, is a free agent, with her first obligations to herself, and though tact should always be exercised in declining any invitation if she means no and nothing short of a sledge-hammer applied to the would-be lover's head will prove it, then by all means lift that hammer.

The third rule, an outgrowth of the foregoing, is a quote from Emerson: "A foolish consistency is the hobgoblin of little minds." Reserve the right to change. Keeping things fluid is, in an affair, as important as keeping an open mind. This is not to say that the relationship should not be taken seriously. It certainly should, and will be, if the partner has been chosen as recommended earlier—i.e., never have sexual relations with a man one would not want as a friend.

As with most codes of etiquette, regardless of the length of the list, it all boils down to simply that good manners are primarily just good sense. Behaving well in an affair is not difficult so long as good judgment is exercised. If such emotional rotten apples as jealousy and resentment get in, then it is time to throw the whole thing out.

Finally, keeping things on an even keel. If the boat starts rocking, reach for a life preserver and take to the water. Keeping things on an even keel is almost impossible, for instance, if chicanery, deception or any of the petty dishonesties so easy to indulge in are not firmly resisted. A good affair occurs only when a strict attention is paid to fairness. That business about all being fair in love and war is downright idiotic if not interpreted as the sad observation that anything goes. That "anything goes" in both is undeniable, but equating love with war is a denial of love as such and concluding that both are means of destruction. Love is *not* war, and when all rules of fair play are discarded in the love relationship, then it has ceased to be love or anything like it. It is unthinkable, for example, to base a friendship on an "anything goes" principle. When a friend becomes deceitful or disliking he is no longer a friend.

There are enough specifics (do's and don't's) in sex-without-marriage protocol to rival the New York telephone directory in listings. But, as with the KAMA, SUTRA, that famous guide-book to sex, who needs it? The practitioners of sex without mar-riage know all the rules to start with, for the language of love has nothing to do with a study of grammar. Love, like art, is a creative thing, and rules and grammar are craft.

CHAPTER ELEVEN

ADULT ORPHANS

WHILE THE lone Wolverine type of woman who lives and loves as she pleases is a sort of societal misfit, she is saved from being an outcast because she is not a burden. She conducts her life with good sense and is independent. There are those who do not, and instead of being truly independent, they are merely stamping their feet and having things their own way—at everybody's expense. These people living outside society's law are adult orphans. Too immature emotionally to be capable of knowing how to conduct themselves, they are nonetheless obliged to because of their chronological age, and are thus in the same position of parentless children in need of guidance.

There are no asylums for the adult orphans. That is to say, there are no institutions for them where they may be housed, clothed, fed and educated, and, heartbreakingly, there are no havens—using asylum in the meaning that it is a sanctuary—for them either. There is no rest for the wicked, and these are society's "wicked"—the non-conformers who can't make it alone, the independent dependents.

What happens to these grown-up infants? Prisons, for instance, are full of them (ironically, so far society's *only* asylum for them) though the bulk of the adult orphan population does not commit crimes and therefore remains on the outside. Like the war orphans in Europe, they tend to huddle together, traveling in packs and bands, getting along as best they can through begging and charity and odd jobs. These human wrecks—and they are that—are precisely like other orphans in that they come from all sorts of backgrounds, and cover the whole range of humanity in appearance, character, personality, intelligence, etc. They can be persons capable of everything or of nothing; they can be from all walks of life from diva to dishwasher, but the one thing they have in common is what all orphans have in common: they need help.

The typical adult orphan is usually attractive, intelligent, talented, goodhearted; if this person is a woman she is often unmarried and unattached (the man is usually AWOL from a wife and usually attached). Both male and female versions live in a state of almost chronic crisis, are broke or nearly, are between jobs or nearly, or are absolutely unemployable and dependent upon family and friends for everything that money can or cannot buy. To mature persons who have more or less made their peace and compromise with life, the adult orphans seem simply unbelievable. Why, they ask in amazement, can't Mary find a job? She's so bright and attractive. Or, why is Mary always broke? Or, why can't Mary settle down with some nice man her own age? The psychologist knows very well why Mary drifts forlornly on the surface of existence, usually tortured by depression, or, when she isn't, in a high tension state of euphoria which is equally unrealistic.

Tragically enough, though the psychologist knows what Mary's problem is, and though therapy has been known to reclaim such people and restore them to a more normal way of life, Mary usually doesn't have the money to seek help, even if she is desperately aware of her own need. And, paradoxically, as she floats from job to job from friend to friend from lover to lover, her craving need for emotional stability increases. She is as insatiable as a nymphomaniac (and often is one, as well) and will drain friendship dry, just as she usually terrifies the men who become involved with her by the desperation with which she clings. Mary more often than not is an alcoholic or a barbituate addict, or will become so. If she does not commit suicide, either willfully or through careless accident, her fate is almost certain to be a tragic one of another kind: losing her sanity completely, ending up on skid row, or living a pathetic existence as an unwanted nuisance in the home of a relative or a former friend. Rarely does Mary find a man who has the stamina or desire to marry her or live with her on a permanent basis, and when she does, her spouse is usually her male counterpart—the blind leading the blind.

Society should be deeply concerned about its adult orphans and free clinics everywhere should be available to them. Since the adult orphan usually drifts to the large city, and since most psychiatrists and mental health experts are located in cities, the problem could be coped with using existing facilities if funds were appropriated for the purpose.

The signs of the adult orphan's neurosis can usually be detected early in life. In all likelihood, Mary was probably a wild teenager, a poor student regardless of her intelligence, head-strong, sexually promiscuous at an early age, rebellious against her family and all adults, and determined to break away. Mary usually marries young and usually marries several times, but is so immature that she cannot accept the responsibilities of being a wife, mother and homemaker, and, full of resentment at being tied down, breaks from these moorings too, and goes off in another directionless direction. The Marys of adult orphanhood are, for obvious reasons, usually connected in some way or other with the arts, or think of themselves as being artistic. The measure of their talent real or imagined has nothing to do with their capacity for production. Mary almost never writes that novel, though she often makes many brief starts, whether or not she has writing ability. Instead she postpones it, dreams about it, and talks about it, and generally behaves as if she were immortal, and this being the case, there is always plenty of time in the future.

Mary customarily remains younger looking simply because she thinks of herself as a Peter Pan. Often she is able to scrape along until she is in her fifties or late forties before she has to face the fact that, like Grasshopper Green, winter has struck her. What happens to her after that is sad indeed; as sad and as bleak as winter often is itself. There will probably be no further spring for Mary.

Sometimes, of course, these lost ancient toddlers are restored to society and even tardily are able to make considerable contributions to it. When this happens it is usually due to the joint efforts of others: family, minister, friends, doctors. Also, sometimes the Johns and Marys receive bad scares and are jolted into the realization that life has almost passed them by. But growing up at any date is difficult, and a determination to grow up at a late one almost impossible. Understandably, it is often easier for the male of the species to make a come-back than for the woman. If there is too much character damage and reputation damage for the woman, she will find that the cold shoulder she receives cannot be warmed up regardless of her efforts. The man, on the other hand, usually receives both sympathy and understanding.

Why this great leakage of human resources should continue decade after decade, century after century is baffling in any age and unforgiveable in this one when human beings are so proud of their enlightenment, their achievements in so many phases of science. If a fraction of the money spent for the space race were diverted to reclaiming derelicts, the space race might be shortened considerably by the additional brains and talent available to it. However, the stress having always been on youth—and in an absolute sense until very recent years when the study of geriatrics began to reveal new facts about the potentials of the old—it will probably be a long time before the public will become convinced that there are better uses for the senile delinquents than the glue factory.

Big Orphan Mary and the Lone Wolverine are, alas, often mistaken for each other, for to the very conservative eye, or the prudish or bigoted one, both have the same habits and both appear totally undisciplined. For this reason, if no other, sexual independence for women is discouraged on the grounds that the sweet young thing, going the way of all flesh, will not have the courage, sense or willpower to leave the primrose path in time. A life of profligacy, self-indulgence and sloth cannot, however, result when the sweet young thing has normal self-respect, down-to-earth objectivity about her own abilities and limitations, and proper assessment of the meaning of all human life and hers in particular. The female adult orphan has none of these things. If and when she acquires them, coming out of her amnesia, so to speak, she will abhor her own past and those shadows who were her companions.

Just as the alcoholic has given liquor a bad reputation, and addicts have given drugs a bad name, so, too, have the adult orphans given independence and non-comformism a pair of black eyes. If sex without marriage is ever to become a healthy and socially acceptable reality, a universally accepted practice, something will have to be done to create an asylum for the adult orphans so that the long finger of disapproval cannot be pointed at them as the primary example of the results of going against the social grain, taking one's own life into one's hands. When that institution is set up, then Mary will probably write that book and *her* sexual habits, with or without marriage, will be happy ones.

WHEN SEX IS SEX

Though Big Orphan Mary can become a call girl or a prostitute, she usually does not because her exalted or otherwise distorted opinions of her own talents, usually artistic aspirations, make the two ideas incompatible. Also, though Mary may be attractive, she may not be aware that she can cash in on the fact. Of course, whether Mary is aware or not, or whether she spends a lot of her time staring at an empty easel or filling it, if she falls in with a pimp or a crowd of girls whose bedrooms are their offices, she may become a whore.

The professional purveyor of sex is, in a way, a cut above Big Orphan Mary, for Mary is just a cut above being a professional beggar, and at least the prostitute earns her own living. This is not to endorse prostitution or to recommend that female adult orphans graduate to this classification but to point out the intrinsic difference in the character structure of the two kinds of mentally disturbed women. A whore, unlike other members of the underworld that parasitically feed on the upper world, may take pride in the fact that she is earning her own living. In a sense, she is not a criminal any more than a homosexual is a criminal, though our laws punish both as if they were: murderers and homosexuals, for instance, can under certain circumstances, be given equal punishment: in the state of Michigan life imprisonment.

But the prostitute who excuses her profession on the grounds that it *is* a profession, that it has in other cultures and other times been a legal one and under certain conditions is actually though secretly legal in this one, is whitewashing something that is basically ignoble and degrading. Proof of this is everywhere; it is currently to be found in the spate of books on the subject of the call girl, mostly written by psycho-therapists who have had such women as patients or who have troubled to make extensive investigations of prostitution and its practitioners. Unlike the joke about the Vassar girl who replies, when asked how she got into the business, "just lucky, I guess," most prostitutes are not happy in their work and long to "get out of the life" as much as many drug addicts long to "kick the habit." Certainly the history of Yoshiwara, Japan's appalling redlight district in Tokyo where legal prostitution existed for hundreds of years and was outlawed only recently, doesn't say much for the cause of legalizing the sale of sex.

It is curious that money taints sex, but it is true; primarily perhaps because trading money for sex is exploitive. The seller more often than not is deprived the right of independent choice, and physical discrimination is not just a human instinct, but also an animal instinct. A cat will bite, claw and scratch if it is forcibly held against its will, or made to live in close contact with other animals it does not like. The whore, especially the one who lives in a house supervised by a madam or some other person to whom she is answerable, more often than not has little or no choice of customers. Therefore, she is a virtual prisoner of her own profession, without even the rights of a cat. Of course, the streetwalker, the camp follower, the single trollop in business for herself or working for a pimp, can afford some freedom of selection, but not much; she may be hungry, or she may be frightened of physical punishment from her procuror. In any event, the life of the woman who sells sex is a sad one, and, even if her earnings are considerable she is seldom capable of real benefit or enjoyment of them.

What kind of woman becomes a prostitute? All kinds outwardly and from all kinds of backgrounds and educational levels. However, their neuroses are usually pretty similar. They are emotionally insecure women, frequently strongly masochistic, very often morbidly frightened of punishment for disobedience, and women whose normal sense of willpower and independence has been disordered since childhood. Prostitutes, especially highly paid call girls, do sometimes manage to "leave the life," and probably more can look forward to that expectation as psychiatry moves ahead.

However, prostitution will always exist, and there will always be those who deliberately seek it or weakly let themselves be led into it, for greed, one of the deadliest of the seven sins, has always afflicted human nature.

Greed has produced that odious female called the Gold Digger in the twenties, and many other names before and since. The Gold Digger is simply a single-minded prositute, tackling one taker at a time, until his financial use is exhausted or his interest in her is. Though she is not first cousin to the Kept Woman, she is to the Kept Man who is actually a gigilo, not a man out of work, or being supported by a woman for some other reason. This aspect of sex without marriage is usually as intolerable to the hard-working whore as it is to the hard-working virgin, for the Gold Digger deliberately forfeits her right of choice for cold hard cash. True, she may choose her partner, but taste and preference are usually secondary rights. The Gold Digger prefers a handsome bank account to a handsome face. And she literally bends her body to her will, as if her will belonged to a stranger.

This female, this hard sister, usually persuades herself that she has some good sensible reason for her self-perversion: to get some capital to go into business for herself, to put baby brother, or her own baby, through college, to save herself from Mama's miserable fate of poverty and a sadistic husband, etc. She prides herself on being brutally frank with herself, on being shrewd, on being strong enough to be hard. Quick money and big money is worth the sacrifice.

In reality, a normal woman who forced herself into gold digging as a way to putting an egg into a nest and feathering the nest at the same time, probably would find the whole business so gallingly repugnant that she would give up the project before any benefits had accrued. Sticking to a nasty task that goes against the moral grain, offends the esthetic sense, is not a habit of the squeamish, or the honest person with "standards." The gold digger either likes her work or doesn't mind it. If she has become innured to it, she is as depraved as a professional murderer, or any whose sense of values has been twisted by habitual malpractice, due to laziness or even seeming necessity.

So much for the corrupters of sex without marriage, for the girls whose unlicensed license should be revoked. Will their misuse of sexual independence serve to continue the discountenance of it by convention? Or will society eventually come of age, cease in itself to be neurotically immature? Judging from the number of books on the subject of sexual independence, at least fifty per cent of which are written by respected authorities who have opinions to which they are entitled by way of experience and training, something is going to come of all this. Books on controversial subjects, of the actual change coming, but if the voices are numerous enough, loud enough, and emanating from those in authority, minority notwithstanding, the change will come. The question is when? What can the individual do to speed it up?

THE RIGHT TO THE PURSUIT OF SEXUAL HAPPINESS

Writing Congressman Bluebeard, Congressman Nobody, Congressman Everybody, and Senator Diehard will not help. It is true that such a body as the Supreme Court could declare a moritorium on all outdated laws having to do with sexual discrimination not compatible with sex as it should be and already is practised in contemporary society, but Fear is one of the best friends of Dogged Belief and adherence to tradition. It is in the public interest, to be sure, to adjust law to practice, if that practice is widespread for sound reasons, or if the practice, law and tradition are *all* unjust, as in the case of racial discrimination, it is essential that legal measures be taken. Here, in the tradition and practice of sex without marriage, a subterranean entity is rising to the surface to be judged on legal grounds. That that entity, now illegal, has been indirectly nourished by other progressive legislation is not to be doubted. If it has become a monster to some, instead of an overgrown child as it is to others, this can be attributed almost directly to the action taken by government in bringing divorce laws more closely in line with human reality, as it exists. That one step further is now needed. And saying that its coming is up to You is absurdly true.

If, after having read this book and others dealing with the same subject, you still think sex without marriage is a bad idea, should be curtailed, not increased or sanctioned, and laws against it should be enforced in the same way that other disagreeable laws, discordant with the will of the majority are enforced, then you could probably present a strong, lengthy and detailed case for sex *with* marriage exclusively and may have already done so. But if your mind was not more or less made up—for personal, religious, or sociological reasons—then the time has certainly come for decisions and vote casting if sexual persecution is to stop, and the right to the pursuit of sexual happiness is to be added to the already impressive list of accomplishments made in our time. Convention's tough old hide has been pierced often, and here and there the light shines through and the air is free to circulate, but there's plenty of fight in the old girl yet. Yawning and saying, "Oh, well, these things always correct themselves eventually," may be true, but this is not the way of progress or its equally vigorous adversaries. There are those would-be zealots and nurses who are willing to work tirelessly to see that the holes in Convention's hide are patched up, that the dying superannuary beast is kept alive, its strong heart pumping.

For the advocate of sexual freedom, sexual freedom for the grandchildren should not be enough. (If it is, it probably means that the children or grandchildren themselves will have done the real digging and building, albeit on the ground inherited from us.) Procrastination is usually selfishness; if one is personally safe against the storm, it is seemingly less urgent to worry about the weather at all, or those caught out in it. But more and more women may find themselves caught out in it, through natural causes—widowhood, desertion, necessary absenteeism, spinsterhood—as well as those created by liberalization of the law. But what, in a practical way, can be done?

Even in these days of so-called equal rights of the sexes, it is understandable that a decent unmarried woman living in a small town might be hesitant in raising even a small public cry for freedom of sexuality for the sexes. The cry, though a quiet and decorous suggestion, may all the same sound strident upon ears more attuned to the horse and buggy's era of social standards than the jet plane's. In which case, the social critic might immediately be branded as a scarlet woman and severely threatened. However, the fact remains that the horse and buggy *are* anachronisms, and so are mores that existed in that day without taking on the additions of the jet age. So the hue and cry is necessary, and if the instigator can be a cheerleader for a team, so much the better. Word of mouth, followed by action, is the course open to all. Variations upon this method are endless: letters to congressmen (after looking up local statutes, state and federal laws to acquaint oneself with what the legal restrictions actually consist of, where changing them would help, etc.) will probably only result in

8

polite acknowledgments—certainly nothing more until the volume of pressure for action is too heavy to ignore; talking with those whose business is or should be the public welfare: doctors, educators, ministers, parents; then talking to the public itself, especially that part of the public most affected: unmarrieds of all groups—widows, teenagers, divorcees, etc. If enough interest and concern is whipped up, its generation may well continue under its own power in one's community and spread to others. Word of mouth has always been the great factor in creating universal opinion. More best sellers were made through talk than through paid advertisement, but *no* best seller ever would have become one if the need for it, real or created, had not been there.

There is an enormous need, an urgent need for action now in the matter of sexual freedom; striking while the iron is hot may bring victory in our time when we can enjoy it too instead of reserving it for one of the uses and benefits of generations to come. Such postponement is on a par with ancestral wistful thinking of the future day when man could fly. If he could have flown too, he should have done so; time and time-saving is an eternal treasure of humanity, for the human life is, after all, only time. So, since we are capable of flight, let us fly. We have been grounded too long by laziness, ignorance, and foolish adherence to that taxiderm of convention which is merely the padded skeleton of the past.

TOMORROW'S PROBLEMS: OUR FAULT OR THEIRS?

Tomorrow's problems are always our fault to some degree, just as every child can logically claim parental blame. But any problems Tomorrow inherits and keeps around under an accusing label, keeping them intact as if they were coveted heirlooms, is Tomorrow's own grief, just as any child who gets his basic neuroses along with Mother's milk should consider any residual remain his own responsibility when Mother's milk is no longer his staple.

If we don't succeed in clearing the air of convention for future generations, they can blame us for our shortcomings, but if we *do* succeed—if sexual independence actually becomes a matter of law as well as fact—we will have done our duty. However, the manner in which such fact and law is accomplished, how long it takes to pass into the traditional pattern, can affect the problems of the future. What could some of those problems of a sexually liberated culture be?

The first that come to mind are divorce increase, abortion, illegitimacy. Statistics already tend to show that these negative outgrowths of a sexually permissive culture would not emerge as Tomorrow's problems, but are actually those of today and well within our own abilities to handle here and now if the larger, over-all problem were sensibly solved. Ideally, before the next turn of the century, legal abortion will exist, and the abortion rate's pulse will steady itself. If there are more alcoholics today, for example, there are few thoughtful people who really lay this increase to the fact that Prohibition ended. Getting it back might immeasurably aggravate the problem existing. Instead, the population has swelled, thus producing more potentials of all kinds, good and bad. With the increase of population also comes increase of living stresses and distresses. The mutations of the future, the alcoholics of the future, the loose women of the future may all resemble their ancestral counterparts, but they will have their own unique qualities good and bad.

Since divorce, abortion and illegitimacy could be and may be prevented from becoming the sexual inheritance of another era, what are some of the hidden threads we might inadvertently leave behind for them to weave into a tangled fabric of problems?

Possibly many of the unacceptable sexual activities we now minimize, such as incest, sexual abuse of children; or those we persistently fail to deal with effectively and realistically, such as prostitution and homosexuality. It might seem incredible to a contemporary mortal visiting as an earth-bound spirit in a hundred years to find things in such a state, but it could happen. But it depends on their culture and what they make of it as much as it depends on ours.

Our concern is merely to leave our bed and board as clean as possible for the next occupant; or as parents say, to do all we can—and that is as much as any departing tenant or parent can be expected to do.